'Author, white male, 47 yrs, 5'7",
inhalation, WLTM readers with GS
WWJD . . .'

Jonathan Clark has been a university chaplain in Bristol and
London, and has worked in theological education in Salisbury.
He is now parish priest of two parishes in Hackney, East
London. He is also Chair of Affirming Catholicism UK, and a
member of the Church of England's General Synod.

THE REPUBLIC OF HEAVEN

A Catholic Anglican Future

JONATHAN CLARK

First published in Great Britain in 2008

Society for Promoting Christian Knowledge
36 Causton Street
London SW1P 4ST

British Library Cataloguing-in-Publication Data
A catalogue record for this book is available from the
British Library

ISBN 978–0–281–05948–5

1 3 5 7 9 10 8 6 4 2

Typeset by Graphicraft Ltd, Hong Kong
Printed in Great Britain by Ashford Colour Press

Produced on paper from sustainable forests

Contents

There are too many people and places who have a share in whatever may be good about this book. I'd like to dedicate it to them all, but it would end up like the notices in church: I'm always forgetting the most important one.

So with thanks and apologies to you all, I'd like to dedicate this book not to the past that produced it, but to the future of which it will be a small part, and in particular to the very last person to read it. You may be researching a PhD in a suitably small corner of early twenty-first-century history, or rummaging through the oddments bin at a second-hand book fair; whoever you are, I hope you, and all your predecessors, have had some joy in picking this up.

1

It's my story

Christianity has died many times and risen again; for it had a god who knew the way out of the grave.[1]

This is a book founded on hope – hope that the future of the Church is brighter than most people imagine. More specifically, hope that the Catholic tradition within the Church of England is not the Church's past, but holds the key to its future engagement with the society in which we live. It probably seems hugely unlikely, even to those within the tradition; for most other Christians it probably sounds like cloud cuckoo land. But whatever you may feel, I'd like to invite you to join me on the journey. Please consider yourself invited into a conversation with me – even if I sadly won't be able to respond to your thoughts as you read. I would take it as a compliment if I pick up a second-hand copy of this book somewhere, and find it full of marginal scribble – even of the 'No! What rubbish!' variety. I write from within the Church of England, and from within British society, from inner urban London – and no doubt all of that shapes what I have to say, but I hope this story will have resonances far beyond. Whether you agree with me or not by the time we reach the end, I hope that you will at least agree that there is reason to hope for the Church, that it can still be the body of Christ for the sake of the world.

So this is a story of the future, a story I am hoping to see come true. But the future I want to suggest for the Catholic tradition is not a straightforward progression from the past, still less a repetition of it. In a world that is continually transforming itself, as ours is, the Church too needs to be continually re-created by the Spirit at work within it. 'The Catholic tradition' in the Church of England is not monolithic, nor static. But right now it needs more than gradual change; some things need to die, and it is only if they do that the ground will be cleared for a renewal. 'See, I do a new thing . . .': the art of discerning futures is not to extrapolate forwards from what is now, but to see what is stirring beneath the surface. The straight-line statistical forecasts for most churches that would describe themselves as Catholic lead to extinction, but where there is death there is also the hope of resurrection, and it is that hope which has led to this book.

The problem with stories of the future, though, is that most of them are mere fantasy – pleasant fun, but you don't bet your mortgage on them. So if my story of the future is to have any credibility it has to be rooted in the past and the present. I want to start this story of the Church at an individual level, with the story of my own spiritual journey. This is partly a gesture of honesty.[2] Most books are autobiographical to some extent; the picture I am painting comes out of my own experience and draws on the various spiritual dwelling places I have found. But perhaps more importantly still, a story of the Church's future, if it is to have any force, needs to be a story owned by individuals within the people of God. It is not a programme for institutional reform. Church structures cannot bring about the realization of vision (though they can do much to hinder it). I am inviting you to see whether this story of the Church's future is one that might also help you to understand your story, different as it will be from mine.

A rough guide to me

Only within the Church of England could I have followed my particular spiritual journey (and even then I nearly fell over the side at one point). At the age of five I started Sunday School in the parish to which we had just moved. It happened that the parish was conservative and evangelical, and the majority of the congregation came to it because their own parish churches were neither. The core of our worship was the twenty-minute sermon, expounding Scripture (I remember we spent nearly a year on 1 Peter). From the beginning, I didn't quite fit. I failed completely to come up with a moment of conversion, and was left arguing that infant baptism had worked for me, which was an unpopular position in a church whose members were mostly in favour of 'believers' baptism' of adults. But even when the rest of the family moved house and parish, I stayed there, because I met with a seriousness about faith, and a commitment to grow in the Christian life, that remain my inspiration – even though I now interpret them very differently. Later on, as a still slightly evangelical ordinand, training for the Church of England's ministry at an evangelical college, I escaped to spend a few days at one of the Anglo-Catholic theological colleges. I loved the worship, and was deeply attracted by the spirituality of the place. What I couldn't stand was the seemingly complete disregard for normal human courtesy between the students. The Christian command to love seemed to have been sublimated into a sphere far above trivial things like how you treat your neighbours. I remain grateful for the naïve assumption in evangelicalism that your faith will make a difference to every part of your life.

The charismatic movement did creep into my home church, through the back door of the youth group. Away from the church's leadership, we had our moments of worship in the Spirit, and I at least found there a way to begin to integrate my feelings into my Christian worship. If the parish church was rather cerebral in its theology (if you think the right thoughts about God, you are saved), then the charismatic experience was quite the opposite (if you feel the right feelings, you're OK). All of that continued through to university, where I ended up as a leading light in the Christian Union and flirted briefly with the house church movement. I wandered back to Anglicanism, though, for a couple of reasons. The first was that, though we were (by definition) supposed to be open to the Spirit of God in the house churches, there was still too much fear to allow the really unpredictable to happen. It was always the leaders (official and unofficial) who spoke in tongues, gave the interpretations, knew when it was time to sing another song. And the pattern was amazingly regular from week to week. House church liturgy was too unchangingly rigid for me. The second was the degree of self-deception and manipulation I saw around me in the Christian Union. With no liturgical or biblical boundaries, it was the charismatic characters (in the non-religious sense of the word) who became arbiters of what was really 'the movement of the Spirit'. I remember once trying to argue that the CU prayer meetings should include some use of English (at the time there was nothing but singing, praying or occasionally shouting in tongues). I was met with the immortal response: 'The problem is, Jonathan, you're in the flesh but we're in the Spirit.' I stopped going to prayer meetings after that, and was left in a bit of a dead end, not quite knowing where I belonged. But it certainly brought home to me that issues of liturgy and of church order are not irrelevant to the life of faith.

Things really began to change later, in my ordination training. The Director of Pastoral Studies had me in to talk about my major placement, and I said, 'I know how successful evangelical parishes work; could I go and work with a successful Catholic parish and see what that's like?' The mythology of evangelicalism is that there's no such thing, but fortunately it is less rooted in fact than some myths, so off I went. That was a huge turning point in my life, though as I'm a stubborn sort of person it took a long time to work itself out. On reflection, what was the key to my sense of spiritual liberation was the bodily nature of Catholic worship. I loved crossing myself, genuflecting, bowing – and once I was ordained priest I loved all the ceremony of presiding at the eucharist. I experienced all

4

these things as a great freedom – freedom from the obligation to think the right thoughts or feel the right feelings. My thoughts wander in many directions, and I quite often come to worship feeling I'd rather still be in bed, but the point is that I'm there, in church, and that is worship in itself. By doing what I do I am expressing the faith that forms my whole life. I know of course that that is just the reverse of some people's experience, and that they have made spiritual pilgrimages into evangelicalism in order to leave what, for them, was a 'dumb ceremony' completely disconnected from faith. I don't want to suggest that that was wrong for them – maybe for you. But it was the pathway in the opposite direction that worked for me.

Over the years since I've been ordained (19 as I write this), I have gradually grown into the Catholic tradition within the Church of England, though without ever feeling that I needed to reject or turn my back on the evangelical part of my experience. I hope I'm not a prissy Anglo-Catholic; I don't really mind if people break the liturgical rules so long as they do so with grace. In fact, I have now come to the conclusion that the rules of liturgy do not exist. Telling someone else they've done it wrong is more like a move in an ecclesiastical game of Mornington Crescent[3] with additional lace and incense.

It was only after having begun to identify myself as an Anglo-Catholic that I began to realize what a quixotic thing it was to do. The Catholic tradition in the Church of England was busy tearing itself in two over the ordination of women to the priesthood. Parishes in the Catholic tradition, with tiny congregations, decaying buildings and mummified liturgy, were being brought to life again by young evangelical clergy. There were even courses run for them, with titles like 'So now you're wearing vestments!', to help them adapt to this strange mission opportunity. I had been introduced to the Catholic tradition in one of its remaining bastions of strength, but I soon realized it wasn't like that for most parishes. In order to understand why, I need to leave my own story here (to be taken up in the next chapter) and give something of my own take on the history of the Anglo-Catholic movement, and the hole it had got into.

A rough guide to Anglo-Catholicism: The up side

The Catholic tradition doesn't seem, to those outside it (or most in it, for that matter), to be in very good shape. But in its origins it embodied, as Geoffrey Rowell's impressive study indicates, a 'vision glorious' of the life and vocation of the Church.[4] It is generally agreed to have begun in 1833, its starting point being a sermon preached by John Keble against the amalgamation, by parliamentary authority, of some Irish dioceses. This may not seem the most likely spark to light a major movement in the Church, but it was only a representative issue. The underlying concern was whether the Church was a religious branch of the state, or whether it was a 'divine society'. If the state had authority to amalgamate dioceses, it had authority over the Church in ordering how it went about its spiritual duties; and it was that principle that the Tractarians opposed. They (and they were called Tractarians because of the tracts they produced) argued for a recovery of the Church from what they perceived as domination by an increasingly secular state. Their 'glorious vision' was for a renewed Church, freed from its bonds, faithful to its calling of worship and pastoral care. As Kenneth Leech[5] puts it, they emphasized 'catholicity and the revival of the sacramental life'[6] – 'catholicity' being perhaps a more appropriate word than 'catholicism', as the early Tractarians were quite unlike their followers, the ritualists. It was with this second generation that the term Anglo-Catholic really began to be appropriate.

Ritualists took on the theological teaching of the Tractarians, and clothed it, increasingly as the nineteenth century went on, with the ritual of the Roman Catholic Church as it was at that time. They did so with great conviction and devotion, and often in parishes serving the worst slums of the industrial cities:

places where the work was hard, risk of disease was high, and the financial rewards low. Flowing out of this commitment to the poor was the tradition of Anglo-Catholic social critique, some of it uncompromisingly socialist, and some more pragmatic and reformist.

At the very height of its strength, the 1933 Oxford Movement Centenary Congress, the key insights of the Catholic Revival in the Church of England were set out like this:[7]

- *The sacramental character of the Church*: the recovery of the belief that God was really involved in the life of the Church through the sacraments, and that therefore they should be regularly and conscientiously celebrated. As was said even then, 'It may safely be said that there are few members of the Church of England, however "moderate" or "Protestant" they may believe themselves to be, whose outlook on the sacraments is not profoundly coloured by the influence of Tractarianism.'[8]
- *The social mission of the Church*: Without claiming it as their exclusive property, Catholic Anglicans manifested their responsibility for society as a whole through their work in the very poorest areas of the country; they placed Christian social responsibility on a firm theological footing through the doctrine of the incarnation, and they saw that human weakness meant that God's grace was needed if people were genuinely to live for one another's good.
- *Personal holiness*: 'Tractarianism in this respect was a reincarnation of Methodism,' believing that 'no one is incapable of sanctity'.[9] It was this that underlay initiatives as diverse as the revival of sacramental confession, the establishment of theological colleges to properly train the clergy for their pastoral duties, and the promotion of retreats and missions (parish missions were an Anglo-Catholic invention).
- *The pastoral authority of the Church*: possibly the most difficult to swallow in an anti-authoritarian age, but key to any creative engagement with the Catholic tradition, now or then.

As Michael Ramsey wrote: 'Individualism has no place in Christianity, and Christianity, verily, means its extinction'[10] – not that Catholic Christianity extinguishes the individual; but it does imply that the individual is not the sole point of authority in relation to his or her own life, which is the end of individual*ism*.

• Finally, where we started with John Keble's sermon, *the Church's spiritual independence.* No-one now would deny that the Church should have control over its own under-standings of what the Christian faith means, and how it should worship – but it was only in 1974 that the Worship and Doctrine Measure finally ceded Parliament's control to the Church's Synod. During much of the early history of the Catholic movement, its opponents were quite content to use governmental power to try to oppose its advance in the Church.

So what went wrong? A tradition that seemed to have so much, that felt in 1933 as if it were the future for the Church of England, had within a few years, so it seemed, fallen into disarray and decay.

A rough guide to Anglo-Catholicism: The down side

It was not accidental that the Catholic movement lost direction; it was disabled by its own inherent difficulties. To contrast with the list above, here is Kenneth Leech's analysis of the weaknesses of Anglo-Catholicism:

> The first is a profound inability to cope with issues of human sexuality, resulting in a dread of women which often reaches the point of real gynophobia. The central problem here lies in the historic and ambivalent relationship between Anglo-Catholicism and homosexuality, a relationship which goes back to the early years of the movement . . .

The second feature is an organic and rigidly hierarchical view of both church and society which veers towards a kind of fascism . . . Many Anglo-Catholics, particularly those of a Papalist outlook, have shared in this view of the social order . . .

However, there is a third serious problem within the Anglo-Catholic culture: its creation of a world within a world. Valerie Pitt has described the growth of Anglo-Catholicism as a type of cultural distortion which deviated more and more from the world of reality. By creating a world within a world, she claims,

> The Tractarians unconsciously made religion a life substitute rather than a life revealer, not a way into the splendours of the visible world but a way out. That habit of mind is fixed in us still, and ultimately it is destructive of religion itself.[11]

To these I would want to add another, maybe so obvious to Kenneth Leech as not to need mentioning: the continual gravitational pull of the Church of Rome, which I'll explore in just a moment. The combination of these factors was enough in the end to drain the positive energy out of the Anglo-Catholic movement, to split it into increasingly small splinter groups, and to leave it where it has been for many years – treading water at best, but mostly in steep decline. If these factors are important still, and I think they are, then any renewed Catholic movement in the Church of England must brace itself to confront them and move on from them.

Right from the beginning, Anglican Catholics had a huge problem with distinguishing Catholicism from Roman Catholicism. The Oxford Tractarians tried to do so, but many in the end were unable to resist the claims of Rome. If the beginning of the Oxford Movement is dated to 1833, it was only 12 years old when it lost its great hero, John Newman, and the steady stream of conversions has continued unabated since then. Newman was eventually won over by the claim of the Roman Catholic Church to be 'the single and authentic representative of the primitive church'.[12] Others have gone in response to individual questions of doctrine (most recently the ordination of women to the priesthood) or for less rigorously theological reasons, but I want to argue that there is one underlying problem, which has shackled those who remain within the Anglican Communion as much as it has drawn those who left. The problem is that there has been a basic acceptance of the Roman Catholic Church's definition of 'Catholic'. Since this has always involved a claim that other Churches are less Catholic, it becomes an interesting problem to accept the teaching and remain in another Church. One of the most interesting ways in which Anglican Catholics have done this is to regard the Church of England as an accidentally detached branch of the Catholic Church, which when the time is right will be re-grafted into its true parent. It is of course somewhat tricky that the Roman Catholic Church has never regarded the Church of England in this light; the Anglo-Catholic capacity for doublethink was wonderfully illustrated by disparaging references to the 'Italian Mission' when the Roman Catholic Church re-established dioceses in England during the nineteenth century.

Sexuality, and particularly homosexuality, is the great unspoken issue within Anglican Catholicism. It is undoubtedly the case that a large number of Anglo-Catholic clergy are homosexual by orientation. As far as I am concerned, that is not a problem. The problem is that Anglo-Catholics have not found a way of confronting the fact – let alone using it as a resource to help them understand their calling within the Church and for the community beyond the Church. It is of course only relatively recently that homosexual practice was de-criminalized in the United Kingdom,[13] and it remains both a legal offence and a social taboo in many parts of the world. Again, the influence of Roman Catholic moral teaching, which has consistently regarded homosexual practice as sinful, may have been as important as anything else: but what I believe might have been a resource in helping the Church (possibly against its will) to confront God's calling in the world was instead swept under the carpet.

Kenneth Leech points towards an 'organic and rigidly hier-archical view of both church and society' as the next reason for the decline in Anglo-Catholicism. This of course stands in contrast to the stream he has represented in the Church of England from the 1960s onwards, of Anglo-Catholic Socialism. Donald Gray[14] describes the succession of groupings within the Church of England up to 1945 which attempted to inspire the Church with a socialist vision of the Kingdom of God – a task which the Jubilee Group would take up in the latter part of the century. But arguably a stronger tradition within Anglo-Catholicism was a Romantic desire for the restoration of a myth-ically happy medieval society, in which the priest's sacramental role was unquestioned and sufficient. The danger was that this became in effect 'a sickly pietism and a right-wing reactionary stance in social and political issues'.[15] On the other hand, there has also been a tendency for some deeply involved in social action to regard the Church's life and worship as somewhat of a distraction from the real task of building God's Kingdom. As one long-term member of the congregation of such a priest said, 'Laity were regarded as an optional extra.' Again, it would seem that there was an inability to keep together the two poles that gave the Anglo-Catholic vision its tension and therefore its life: poles expressed in the famous speech of Bishop Frank Weston at the 1923 Anglo-Catholic Congress: 'You cannot claim to worship Jesus in the Tabernacle, if you do not pity Jesus in the slum.'[16]

Ken Leech's final point exposes the reason why the ordina-tion of women to the priesthood was such a decisive moment for Anglican Catholics, and disastrous for many. It wasn't merely important in its own right, but it brought into the open the ambiguity inherent in the world-view of many Anglo-Catholics. The decision to ordain women to the priesthood was an inescapable manifestation of the Church of England's belief that it did in fact have the authority to make such decisions. Many rejected the principle, and the decision, and left; but for many others it merely heightened the tension without resolving it. Moving to 'safe' dioceses, or opting out of the normal diocesan system into the care of flying bishops, provided a sort of expedient. But the very fact that many were prepared to do something as 'un-Catholic' as opting out of the authority of their own diocesan bishop, in order to remain within the Church of England, only added to the contradictions and unhappiness within the tradition.

If you were to ask me, before I had become one, what Anglo-Catholics were like, I would have offered a fairly confused picture. As far as I can now recall it would have included these elements: people who didn't really believe in mission, who spent too much time fussing over inessentials, who seemed to believe most of the right things (along with a whole lot of irrational extras) but didn't know how to live them out in such a way that people would want to attend their churches. Maybe I'm just being kind to myself, because I think I was partly right. In particular, much of Anglo-Catholicism had retreated into its own little world, a world full of precise distinctions and obscure disagreements which bore increasingly little relation to the world outside. It is a world that still exists, ever shrinking, but still largely filling the niche in the wider Anglican Communion labelled as 'Catholic'.

But in a much more important way I was completely wrong. It is true that 'Anglo-Catholicism' is pretty much identified with the sorts of issues and problems I've outlined above, but there are many Anglo-Catholics who aren't. The label has become attached to those who appeal to the past, who find almost all change impossible to countenance, and who are unable to confront the contradictions in the tradition outlined above. But there is (and always has been) an alternative tradition which has never been regarded as properly Catholic (by the more traditionalist), but has I think been where the real life of the tradition has always lain. Though some are identified with either extreme, we're not talking about two completely separate camps here. To take the most obvious case: there are some in favour of women's ordained ministry who are in other ways very reluctant to think about change, and others who will experiment with almost anything – but remain opposed to that decision.

It is of the nature of flowers to die after they have done their reproductive duty for the whole plant, and one could argue that the final great gift of the Catholic tradition to the Church of England as a whole was also tied up with its death as a lively separate movement in the Church. George Carey noted, speaking as Archbishop of Canterbury to a conference of Affirming Catholicism, that 'partly due to its own success Anglican Catholicism seems to have lost its sense of direction these days. And indeed, its obsession with the single issue of the ordination of women seemed almost to indicate a deathwish.'[17]

But it is not merely the case that the Catholic movement had made its glorious last gift to the Church before reaching its happy end. As Geoffrey Rowell puts it:

> [M]any of the insights, Catholic and critical, to which the Catholic movement witnessed had been absorbed and become part of the lifeblood of the Church. If it is difficult to write the history of the Catholic Movement in Anglicanism after [1948], it is partly because this is the case, though partly also because of a certain theological failure to reinterpret the Catholic tradition in a living and creative way. The Catholic revival in Anglicanism must, like all movements . . . change in order to remain the same.[18]

Another vision – a new beginning?

That has been the problem. The Anglo-Catholic movement – or a large part of it – has never wanted to confront the future enough to pay the price, which is change. Ironically, this was pointed out even in the glory days of 1933: 'We shall do no good with easy truisms or trite platitudes or unintelligent repetitions of age-old *formulas*. The only authority which men will respect . . . is an authority which, however firmly it bases itself upon the proved truths of the past, is vivacious enough to bring them into vital contact with the ever-changing moods of the present.'[19]

There have always been those who do want to bring change – but the movement as a whole has not gone with them. The long story of Anglo-Catholic Socialism[20] is one prime example: despite its profound engagement with the interface between faith and the fate of society, it did not succeed in dislodging the inward-looking and often politically reactionary culture of much of the movement.

I believe we need to be even more radical, to go even deeper, to re-understand what 'Catholic' means if we are to realize its potential for the future of the Church. The invitation is there – the way has been pointed out already:

Some time ago I copied a few lines of verse from a friend's bulletin board:

They drew a circle that shut me out
Heretic, rebel, a thing to flout.
But love and I had the wit to win
We drew a circle that took them in.

Is not this what a truly Affirming Catholicism would do? It would bring out of its treasures things new as well as old, and it would see grace in the conflict of ideas and human types. It would draw a circle large enough to include the world that God loved so much that he sent the divine Son into it to affirm its preciousness and die for its freedom. Such a Church would be a church of sinners and surprises – of sinners, because it would be for the not already perfect. It would be for men and women on the way, knowing something of their strength and much about their weakness. It would be a Church big enough to hold the ones whose ritual status is allegedly not quite perfect, because they have failed some test of acceptability, by their marital or sexual status, or by their inability or refusal to see the point of pretending to exact knowledge of the unknowable mystery that besets us, yet who want to accompany the tradition and, above all, share its experience of prayer and silence. But above all it would be a Church of surprises because it knew that God had not finished yet and no grave can hold the divine.[21]

2

My other story:
Postmodern *and* Catholic

Catholicity is not . . . an attainment, so much as a quality of mind;
it cannot be possessed, but it can be hungered after. It is not the
opposite of anything, except of opposition and exclusiveness.[1]

A bit more about me

Moving to London a few years ago, I took advantage of the
comparative freedom I had as a university chaplain to try
out a variety of churches and groups. While I was doing so, I
stumbled across Holy Joe's, a group which at that time met in
the upstairs room of a pub in Clapham, usually for discussion,
but monthly for worship. I suppose most of its membership
had been part of evangelical churches at some time, and now
definitely weren't. That was about as definite as things got: Holy
Joe's was never a group that had mission statements or plans
of action. It happened, and did things very well, but with a style
which allowed for the widest possible range of views, in which
people were allowed to be themselves and wander around,
protest against or explore more deeply the Christian faith.

The part of Holy Joe's that had the greatest effect on me
was the 'Sacred Space' worship events, and particularly the
Midnight Masses that the group produced at Greenbelt[2] in the
late 1990s. They took a huge amount of effort, and not a little
emotional angst, but some of the results were amazing. For
the benefit of those who have never experienced alternative
worship, this is the sort of thing I'm talking about:

White paper leaves glowed starkly under the sole illumination of blacklight as we carried them to the beautifully sculpted wire tree and tied the ribbon to its branches. The Tree of Life bore our prayers as we knelt on one of seven cushions in a circle around a low white-gravel covered circular altar, incense drifting among us, electronic music carrying the mood. The priest intoned the words of the Great Thanksgiving, and we responded, 'Holy, Holy, Holy, the Lord God almighty, who was and is and is to come'. Bread and wine and a white stone were put in our hands. White clothing and papers glowed as they passed the blacklight. We reflected on our lives – explored or unexplored? Scripture was read. 'Unto the one who prevails I will give a white stone' (Revelation 2.17). A spoken meditation guided our private ones. We worshipped. We met with God.

This took place in a large room without seating, with a bare minimum of décor – the tree, the altar and surrounding cushions – and lit only by altar candles, five blacklight tubes and spill from two slide projectors carrying unchanging scripture texts. Two hundred and fifty people packed the space, sitting on the floor. It would have been just as moving if only six people had been present. This is new worship or alternative worship at its best.[3]

Each time, as we prepared the worship, the most surprising thing to me was the lack of privilege given to texts. The words might very well come after the visual images had become clear. The wire tree and its white leaves were not an illustration of a meaning that had been decided in advance: they were the meaning, whatever it was that people made of them. What was done was placed in the context of the biblical and liturgical traditions of the Church: this was a eucharist recognizable in form to anyone from the mainstream Churches; but the tradition had not dictated everything. For me, this was about the risk of allowing the Holy Spirit to be at work.

I was reminded of the contrast with my earlier experience of worship in the house church movement: in helping to prepare Sacred Space, I found myself for the first time experiencing the creativity (as well as the uncertainty and vulnerability) of a body in which power was not controlled from the top. Certainly meanings were not dictated; what the worship meant to one person was not controlled by an authorized version of what we were doing, a definitive interpretation coming from above.

As we worked on the Masses, we used symbols, rituals, texts from a wide range of backgrounds, but in common with many other alternative worship groups we had mined quite deeply into the Western Catholic tradition, while avoiding anything that seemed to tie down individual actions to particular meanings (let alone doctrines).

The principles I felt we were working with were something like this (they were never articulated): traditional texts and actions are resources, not rules; visual images, and the other senses, are much more prominent; leadership functions differently – by articulating consensus rather than dictating truth; people can think their own thoughts about what's going on; and engagement with the resources of contemporary culture is a natural part of the worship.

These things are not just applicable to acts of worship; for me they indicate a change in the whole way of being church. What we do in worship reflects what we really think about the life of the Church as a whole. My experiences of alternative worship led me to think not just about the eucharist, but about how the Church relates to the culture of which it is part.

Spirituality on the Holloway Road?

The university of which I was chaplain was not a posh institution – it had started as the Northern Polytechnic, was for quite a while North London Poly, somewhat briefly the University of North London, and is currently incarnated as one of the constituent parts of London Metropolitan University, which sounds so much better. A typical student might be a woman of African

Caribbean origin in her 30s with a couple of children, who had left school with few qualifications but was now beginning to use her intellectual abilities to get a qualification. The place was not an ivory tower, nor somewhere the chaplain had a cosy institutional cocoon within which to operate. Insofar as one can be while being paid by the Church, I was on the margins, and I think in a good place to see how irrelevant and unimportant religion was becoming, except among the radical Muslims. It wasn't that I met opposition so much as surprise that the Church was still hanging around when clearly no-one needed it any longer.

Before this I had read quite a lot of contemporary philosophy, which I'm going to try to use as a way of explaining the situation I was in (and the situation the Church is heading towards as well) – and the reason why a new kind of Catholic revival is needed. I was walking down the Holloway Road (not an activity recommended without a gas mask), past the fetish boutique, when I saw a poster for the Manic Street Preachers' album *This is my truth tell me yours*. And I thought – here it is: contemporary philosophy hitting HMV. Or more accurately, what the philosophers had been perceiving, now becoming quite naturally also part of everyday culture, through the most pliable and responsive medium, contemporary music.

In lyrics like the Manics' we are confronted with a world that is still strange and new for most of the Church, but is simply home for a large percentage of the population as a whole. This is my truth, tell me yours, says: we live in a world full of stories, but I don't have any equipment for saying which of them is 'true'. Maybe that's not the most important question any more. Everyone has an individual account to give, and many of those accounts make claims about how the world is, what it means to be a human being, the purpose of life; and, as ever, they contradict each other. The defining point about contemporary society which merits the label 'postmodern' is that there is no way of positioning these stories in a hierarchy, no way of judging which one is the best, the most real, the true; and that is because people can't even agree on the ground rules for making such a decision.

If there's no foundation, no hierarchy of truths, you can start from anywhere in explaining the world, even a rock group's album title. Let me show my age: *The Hitchhiker's Guide to the Galaxy* includes a machine which can extrapolate the entire universe from any one part of it: in that case, a piece of fairy cake. In a self-deprecating and very English way, Douglas Adams was making the same point that post-structuralist philosophers had been making in very difficult French: everything is connected to everything else in the world of human discourse, and nothing has the privilege of being the one sole starting point, the thing that explains everything else. You can start from anywhere, because any starting point is always part of the argument. This may cause problems for God – but only if you believe that human beings can really understand God. The God in whom I believe is always beyond anything human reason can understand: the word that undergirds all of creation is not a word spoken or understood within the world itself. So any attempt to ground an understanding of the world from any one part of it is heresy (to use a word that doesn't often pass my lips).

But starting from fairy cake might take a while, so I'm going to use one of those much abused phrases that keep on recurring in books like this because they do sum up very neatly the changes that have happened, are beginning, or still lurk on the horizon (depending on where you are in the social geography of Western culture). My starting point is the phrase coined by Lyotard: 'incredulity towards metanarratives'.[4] This phrase has been read in many different ways, and incorporated into many different perspectives on contemporary society. Adding to the list of interpretations, I would like to use it as a jumping-off point for explaining the postmodern times in which we live. As I explain what it means to me, it may become clear why there are so many interpretations of postmodernity.

Incredulity towards metanarratives / An incredulous society

Metanarratives are the 'big stories': the stories that claim to make sense of the world as a whole, to provide a framework for human living within which the individual stories of our own lives, and the collective stories of our communities, can take shape. They are the stories of Marxism, or Islam, or Christianity – or even postmodernism. Lyotard argues that we have come to a point at which such claims are met with incredulity: it is impossible for many people to believe that there could be one over-arching story which could make sense of everything. It's not a question of believing that the Christian story (or any other story) is wrong: it's an inability to believe that there could be any such thing as a metanarrative. I nearly wrote 'refusal to believe', but that's the point. It's not that people in postmodern times make an intellectual argument that rejects metanarratives for certain logical reasons. The point Lyotard is making is rather that metanarratives are not even part of the mental furniture with which people approach the world. No-one bothers arguing against the existence of flying elephants (except of course for Dumbo); metanarratives are entering the same world of ideas which are clearly complete fantasy.

If metanarratives are dead or dying, what takes their place? Little stories, ideas from here or there, individual experiences: in postmodern times people construct their identity from whatever material comes to hand and seems to fit. It may not make a pleasingly logical structure; it may have gross inconsistencies or elements that are (to everyone else) clearly false: but it is my truth, your truth, and there is no standpoint from which I might say to you (or vice versa), 'That's wrong.' To do that implies common standards of judgement, which implies a common world-view, a metanarrative.

Stretching Incredulity

So here I was enjoying Holy Joe's, and also on Sundays happily worshipping in an Anglo-Catholic parish, and working on the Holloway Road, and feeling strongly that these worlds had something to say to each other. I felt no contradiction between the two different worshipping worlds I inhabited, and the cultural setting I was part of, but I realized I was in a very small minority. It seemed obvious to me that each had something the other lacked, and I began to think that some sort of conversation between the three might be the catalyst for the Church as a whole to move on, and to re-engage with the world in which I was working.

So my experience of being a Catholic Anglican, and of being part of Holy Joe's, and working in university chaplaincy in an ex-polytechnic in inner London, and trying to understand what on earth was going on in society and for the Church, led me to feel that in all that somewhere there was the potential for a renewed Catholic way of looking at what it means to be the Church. The postmodern is a bit like Serleena in *Men in Black II*: a creature apparently solid and whole, but in fact capable of becoming a multitude of intertwining snakes, always liable to slide off in a new direction. The defiant solidity of traditional church has little to say to such a strange creature.

But yet it is as a Catholic (from within the Church of England) that I define myself. What possible points of contact are there for those of us who find ourselves within the mainstream Churches? Must we either give up everything that makes our own identity recognizable to ourselves, or alternatively live as rejectionists in postmodern times, forlornly clinging on to dying ways of believing? Of course not – the book's only just started, there has to be more to it than that. But if there is to be more for the Churches than a slow death, there will need to be radical surgery.

The reason why is pretty obvious, given the ways in which I have described the Catholic tradition. Whether Roman Catholic or Anglican, the Catholic tradition has up to now been resolutely 'solid'. To take another example of what has been perceived to make it tick, let me quote from a long-dead bishop; the first category that Charles Gore[5] used, and which rings true to me, is 'Tradition', 'which lies behind the New Testament, which found in time legitimate expression in the Catholic creeds, and which made its appeal to the Scriptures'.[6] How can that possibly be reconciled with the de-centred, liquid, eternal present of postmodernity?[7] Past and future are discredited in favour of the continually repeated spectacle of the present: tradition is by definition dead.

The second characteristic is nearly as bad: 'the sacraments, in which all who would be Christians were bound to participate – which were divinely given and necessary instruments of spiritual grace and at the same time, as being ceremonies of the society, bound the spiritual life of its members into that visible fellowship'.[8] The sacramental structure appears to make two claims which are completely unacceptable to postmodern ears. One is that there is a clear and unambiguous channel running between the heavenly and earthly realms, through which divine grace can be guaranteed to flow. The other is the power claim, that all Christian people must engage in this way with these activities, or they're not part of the community any more. Sin becomes defined not only in moral terms – which is difficult enough to justify in an individualistic age – but even in terms of ritual activities. It is a sin not to attend Mass on Sundays: a phrase more likely to provoke amusement than alarm.

Finally comes 'the apostolic ministry, which all must accept, instituted by Christ in the persons of the Twelve and continued in the succession of the bishops down the ages, linking the different churches together by the fellowship of the bishops throughout the world and binding the succession of generations to the apostolic original'.[9] Here we have nothing but a structure of power relationships, tying the people of God into a hierarchical and complete submission. The 'apostolic ministry' seems to function for Gore almost as a spiritual police force, so that any believer is unavoidably bound up into a hierarchical system extending through space and time, conserving the original message of the apostles and policing that preservation among the faithful.

A Catholic way of being that lives within postmodernity is going to be radically different from what the Church has been used to up to now. If we are to retain a sense of identity as church, and also find ways of letting our vision of church evolve, without simply abandoning our past, we'll have to dig very deep: but if we do, I believe the connections are there which can revitalize the tradition even within a postmodern society – and in fact offer the good news of Christ to that society in a way that makes it meaningful, without reducing its challenge.

Deep postmodernity

It may be true that metanarratives are met with incredulity. But of course the argument is circular: to make such a claim is in its own way to construct a metanarrative, a way of explaining 'the way the world is'. And that is where Jacques Derrida comes in; he has made a speciality of holding this paradox, that we can't help making claims to truth, even if we're also admitting that such claims are impossible.[10]

One of Derrida's most famous and misunderstood phrases is that 'there is nothing outside text'. Text, as he uses the word, is all there is. By this he doesn't mean we're all part of a book, or that there's no such thing as the physical world of which we're part. He's talking – as I suppose you might expect a philosopher to do – about the world of meanings and beliefs, the frameworks we use in order to understand the world.

Derrida's claim is that the whole of our understanding of the world we live in is conditioned by the networks of meaning by means of which we make sense of the world: the metanarratives and little narratives we tell ourselves. Those narratives are exactly that – they are stories, texts. They relate to the real things of the world around, but not transparently. We see through a glass, darkly: all we see are the interpreted realities that our textual worlds allow for.

Even more importantly, there is no one-to-one correspondence between the meanings we attribute to things and events, and the things themselves. Meaning is constructed through the relation between networks of possibilities, which can lead off in any number of directions: the possibilities of interpretation are endless. If you've ever given a talk or preached a sermon you will know this if you've received feedback from the listeners; the variety of different meanings that people receive are wonderfully different from each other, and from the message that you as the speaker thought you were putting across. They have become integrated into each listener's own prejudices, concerns and understandings and have taken on a life completely of their own.

The meaning of words is always slipping away: we can't hold it in our hands or our minds, because it runs through our fingers like sand. Even if we were to say 'it's the original author's meaning that counts', how are we to know everything that was going on in another person's mind? If we are honest, we have to admit we don't know everything that's going on in our own. As I type now, I am trying to keep the flow of this argument clear in my head – while not knowing exactly where it will go next. I'm also wondering whether I've remembered to put the bins out, and reflecting on some family issues I'm not going to share with you. Do you need to know those things in order to understand what I am writing? If so, I should provide a personal commentary to every line, and preferably the comments from a couple of psychoanalysts as well. The idea of running down 'the true meaning' of any text is a chimera: the mythical creature that lured unwary travellers to their doom. All we can ever do is enter into dialogue with the texts that come before us. Note that Derrida does not (it seems to me) do what he has been accused of: he doesn't say: 'Well, nothing means anything any more.' He lives with the paradox that we are continually making meaning, but that we cannot control the meaning we have made. It won't be tied down.

Living with paradox, of course, should be something that Christians are good at: we believe in Trinity and incarnation, so why not a few more impossible things before breakfast? We are used to recognizing that human language cannot express the realities in which we nevertheless believe. But we've always tended to be rather uncomfortable about it: we regard it as something of a failing, an embarrassment. Look at how much ink has been spent (and blood spilt) over understandings of both those doctrines. The invitation extended by Jacques Derrida (the Algerian French Jew) is to be free of the impossibilities that we have laid upon ourselves.

Can we possibly take up the invitation? It requires setting aside the desire to make 'the greatest story ever told' into a story that can dominate all others; if not now through inquisition and conquest, at least through telling a story that can beat all the others in town. Because if all stories are linked to all other stories, there's no way that any one of them can claim to be the original and the best: how would such a claim be substantiated? Where can you stand in order to make the argument? All texts – including that one, and this one – are linked into all the others.

In which case we will need to re-examine the characteristics I unearthed from Charles Gore, to see if there are other ways in which they can be understood. We need to think again about what it means to be Catholic.

Not Catholicism but Catholicity?

We live in a world not of truths but of stories. No one of this world's stories (even the Christian one) can extricate itself from the network of other stories: Derrida's net remains in place. In which case what do we do? Shout louder? Put our fingers in our ears to prevent ourselves from hearing the other stories, in case they might be too convincing? Unfortunately these seem quite popular tactics. But I hope I can hint at a less inadequate way (apologies to St Paul).

We can't speak in the tongues of angels and understand one another: if we speak in human languages we immediately descend into the babel of postmodern times. But I want to suggest that this isn't quite such a disaster for theology as we might initially feel. On the contrary, perhaps it is the very desire to speak straightforwardly about God that is the unorthodox snare, brought on us by attachment to the very modernist methodology that ended up with atheist nihilism.

In the incarnation of Christ, God gives Godself to the world in order to save the world. But that act has consequences for God, as well as for the whole created order. In the incarnation, God in Christ becomes part of the world of endless interpretation, the world of multiple possibilities, the world of stories. To try then to tell the story of Christ as if it were outside the world of other stories, as a 'master narrative' that dominates and overpowers other stories, is to miss the point of what God has done for us. A Christian metanarrative is not one that claims power, but one that allows itself to be told in other peoples' stories – that sacrifices its own claims to authority, just as Jesus before his accusers was dumb.

Later on I'm going to talk quite a bit about the theological idea lying behind all of this: *kenosis*, a Greek word meaning 'emptying'. It's been used a lot to talk about what happened at the incarnation, and particularly how we can meaningfully think of Jesus as both human and divine – how is the human not overwhelmed by divinity? Here's a rather complicated quotation:

> [K]enosis is not a self-limitation and not a self-renunciation on God's part; it is the self-realization of the self-surrender of the Son to the Father in the Trinitarian life of God. By virtue of limitless love, the inner life of the Trinity takes its impress from the reciprocal kenosis of the divine persons in relation to one another . . . Kenotic self-surrender is God's Trinitarian nature, and is therefore the mark of all his works 'outwards' (the creation, reconciliation, and redemption of all beings).[11]

Which is to say that it is part of the nature of God always to be pouring out love, Father, Son and Holy Spirit towards one another, and towards the whole creation. It is that pouring out that we see especially in the life, death and resurrection of Jesus, and which we are called to live out.

There is something about Jesus that cannot be given totally into any of the world's stories, because the creative power of God at work within him cannot be controlled into any narrative. In the incarnation power is dispersed, given away, eternally diffused but never exhausted. Its source, Jesus, can't be definitively located within our world, but nevertheless walked upon it and is still known in it, through the sacraments and the work of the Holy Spirit.

In a world dominated by power plays and violence, it is in the recurring hints of something else that we see the continually disappearing face of God – which as soon as we fix it is no longer God's face. Even the Church's story of God cannot claim for itself a definitive and absolute hold on the revelation of God in Christ, because that is not something that the world can contain at all. All our writing, theologizing, preaching, point to something which our words cannot contain.

The resurrection, from this perspective, can serve as the great reminder that there is always more to Jesus. However tightly we might feel we have him sealed in the coffin of our theology, he will undoubtedly roll away the stone and move on ahead of us. There is always another side to his story that our story isn't telling; he will always return to haunt our stories which both tell his story and exclude him from it.

Of course this is still a metanarrative claim (we all make them): the claim that Jesus explodes and subverts whatever metanarrative we might put into words with the love of God which is beyond our language. But it is at least a metanarrative that undoes its own claims to uniqueness as quickly as it makes them; it points always beyond itself.

If this is the story we are living, what does it mean for the way we live – as church, as Christians – within the Catholic tradition? It will mean a complete overhaul of the way in which Catholic Christianity has traditionally expressed itself – which is not an abandoning of Catholicity but a recovery of it in a new context. It's that conjunction that I'm trying to create (though not to complete); a new ground for thinking about what it means to be Catholic in the contemporary world. We'll keep on coming back to it, leaping dangerously from the world of postmodern thinkers into the life of the Church and back again. Fortunately, there are others who have done it better than I, and I can take a piggy-back on their efforts.

John Habgood, as Archbishop of York, gave a lecture entitled simply 'Catholicity'. In it he cleared the ground for thinking again about the Catholic tradition, by distinguishing between Anglo-Catholicism and Anglican Catholicism: the first the party within the Church, the second a way of thinking about the Church as a whole. Or in his own words:

> Of course the connections between the two are intimate and complex. The influence of the Oxford Movement, through the growth of Catholic practices and the absorption of a Catholic spirit, brought about the transformation of the Church of England. But that great achievement owes a huge amount to those Anglo-Catholics who were prepared to press on beyond the limits of the acceptable, and who found their ultimate authority

and rested their ultimate hopes, not in Canterbury but in Rome. Yet . . . their very successes sowed the seeds of their own destruction. To the degree that it remained a movement which restored Catholic consciousness to the Church of England as a whole, the Catholic movement could remain true to its vision and gradually lose its distinctiveness. But as a party within the Church of England, locating much of its authority in another church, it was and is in danger of succumbing to intolerable ambiguities.[12]

We need then to think again about the meaning of tradition, sacraments and ministry from the point of view of a Catholicity which is not tied to Anglo-Catholicism as a party movement, or the dogmatic positions of Roman Catholicism.

Just as a prelude to the next few chapters, here are some sketches of how the traditional language of Anglo-Catholicism might be transformed – without, in my view at least, becoming any less Catholic.

'*Tradition*' is only one way of translating the Latin word *traditio*; the other is 'treason'. The process of handing on, handing over, can be both a way of conserving something and a way of betraying it. I'd want to argue that there has to be some treason in order to be faithful to tradition. Merely to receive something from the past, and pass it on as if it can still function in the same way in a changed society, is not to be faithful at all. If a tradition is to continue to be faithful to its own roots, to convey the same message, it has to change. That means that we have to work with what we have received, engaging with the Scriptures, reflecting on what we have been given, but also trusting to the Holy Spirit's movement in learning new things.

Sacraments, and the problem of counting. The traditional Anglican answer is that there are two – baptism and eucharist – while the Roman Catholic Church numbers seven. Re-understanding sacraments from a postmodern perspective can help us to move away from numbering the ways in which

God is at work. Sacrament can become a way of thinking about how God is at work in the world, how the presence of God is diffused and dispersed into the world God loves. Far from being points of control, the withholding of which excludes people from God's presence, the sacraments as such are pointers towards the sacramentality of all things: specific places through which the presence of God which is everywhere is felt in a specific time and event.

In which case, what of the ministry in the apostolic line, the *priesthood* most definitely not of all believers, but given specifically to bishops, and shared by them with priests, the life-line of salvation stretching back unbroken through the physical guarantee of the moment of ordination, all the way back to the apostles themselves? Sounds wonderful – though all but the most assiduously blind recognize that we have no evidence for the existence of such an unbroken tradition – and even if it is unbroken, some of the hands through which it has passed should have been wielding pickaxes on the chain gang rather than chalices in church. As a Catholic, I do believe in a distinctive priestly ministry to which some are called: but they (we, I) are not called in order to do things to the rest of the Church, or even for the rest of the Church. Ministry exists in order to provoke, challenge, encourage, cajole – whatever it takes to get the church to live up to its calling. Priests are called to open the way so that all can walk in it. If they block the doorway instead, there's no use for them (us, me).

> [I]n the long term, the future lies with Catholicism. It must, because only Catholic tradition is rich enough and stable enough to be able to offer something distinctive to the world without being captured by the world. But it must be a Catholicism which is true to its highest vision, and hence broad enough, hospitable enough, rooted sufficiently in sacramental unity, confident enough in its inheritance to be able to do new things, diverse enough, and yet passionately enough concerned about unity, to be genuinely universal.[13]

alt.catholic

I started this chapter with a description of an 'alternative worship' service of which I was part. That led naturally, for me, into some thoughts about the nature of contemporary society, and right into the clash between that society and the 'solid' church we're still used to being. I've tried to provide above a theoretical argument that there's no contradiction between being Catholic (if you go deep enough into the roots of the tradition) and engaging creatively and positively with a postmodern world. There's still the question of how to do it. That's where we return to where this chapter started.

I am going to claim that the Church is called by the Holy Spirit to embrace a renewed Catholic tradition, using the insights of postmodern thinkers, and some of those communities of faith that are already living out of a postmodern view of the world. The strength of what has been explored through the alternative worship movement now needs to be brought back 'in house' as God's gift to the Catholic tradition.

The challenge is exemplified in the first of the things I learned from alternative worship at Holy Joe's: traditional texts and actions are resources, not rules. In preparing liturgies, 'What works?' is the crucial question, not 'What is the right thing to do?' Alternative worship groups are not looking to reinforce 'correct' belief, or lead worshippers into a charismatic experience of being filled with the Spirit; but even though the aims might be undefined, the pragmatic principle remains. 'What can be used in order to make this act of worship work?', that's the question. If it's something from the Christian tradition, that's fine, but there's no reason to think particularly hard about where it originated, where it fits in the traditional liturgical pattern, and so on. An individual liturgical piece can be freely lifted and used, along with newly created images, texts or liturgical actions. By the same token, newly composed elements of liturgy need not be subjected to too close a theological scrutiny. They are after all temporary, experimental, designed to provoke a reaction rather than dictate a belief: they shouldn't be made to bear too much weight. So from within an alternative worship framework, there's no problem about lifting aspects of the musical and visual culture into a worship context; it doesn't mean that those songs or pictures are now to be regarded as statements of Christian teaching. They serve a purpose once or twice and then are discarded. A Catholic tradition which has spent many years engaged in liturgical archaeology needs to rediscover the virtue of the present-day and the ephemeral! But this pragmatism has a self-limiting tendency; it isn't designed to produce services that will bear repetition. As a movement which indulges in liturgical DIY around the edges of what is established and mainstream, it will always create temporary spaces for worship (physical, emotional or spiritual). For the ongoing encounter with God at depth and every day, the Catholic tradition's historical resources of ritual provide the essential counterpart – so long as the people of God can still connect with them.

The same dialogue applies to the whole life of the Church. Our attitudes towards the priesthood and other ministries in the Church, our approach to the world we try to serve, our attitudes to ethical and moral dilemmas: all of them are challenged by the approach to church life embodied in alternative worship; but the tradition is still vitally important if new insights are genuinely to transform the Church.

The Catholic tradition in the Church of England needs to rediscover itself on new grounds, still just as Catholic, but thinking very differently about what it means to be Catholic. We need to slaughter the sacred cows that prevent us from seeing our own richness and potential vitality, we need to re-read our history completely without the rather sad tendency to ride on the coat-tails of Roman Catholicism. In short, we need freedom from being the slaves of tradition, along with the respect and depth of understanding that have been the traditional prerogative of Catholics. Tradition has to retain a capital 'T', because it isn't merely a historical archive but the gift of the Holy Spirit to the Church in the present. It's not as if the traditional forms of worship are dead, but they need to be connected into a wider vision of worship which includes not just them but also the things I was experiencing in Holy Joe's and on the Holloway Road.

I'm more naturally inclined to read books than to write them, but in the end I felt compelled to write this book. It is an attempt to set out what it would mean for the mainstream of church life to respond to a postmodern culture while remaining authentic to itself. What a response might be will take up the rest of the book. It would mean another of those shifts of perception that come along every now and again in the Church's life, as elements that have been downplayed or ignored take again a more prominent role. It would not mean a return to any previous way of doing things. If there is to be resurrection, there has to be death first, which is a principle that applies all the way through the theological spectrum. If we are to have a renewed (even resurrected) Catholicism, we must be able to recognize that the old has had its day. Solemn Masses will (I hope and trust) continue – but maybe they will be seen as one way of worshipping, rather than *the* way.

So now it's time to use the theological rationale I've set out in this chapter as I try to plot out different ways of living as church, in the light of my understanding of the postmodern times in which we live. Doing that will be a violent process of collision between the culture of our times and the Catholic tradition, and there will be casualties. Some of the 'sacred cows', the things that are so self-evidently right that they can't possibly be changed, will have to go. In order not to leave us with nothing but a bloody shambles (and the makings of a great barbecue), I'll also try to show what I think we might do in order to remake ourselves into a Church that has something to do in postmodern times. Not something to *say to* postmodern times: as if we could stand outside and make pronouncements. Something to *do*: a way of living as church for and within the society of which we are still (just) part. But first I'll have to deal with one more little problem Catholics have: power.

3

Power and how to lose it

On knowing when (and what) to give up

The London Diocesan Synod discussed the remarriage of divorcees. The meeting was held in the Church of St Bartholomew
the Great, Smithfield, among medieval pillars in a holy gloom
which seemed more fitted to a scene from *The Name of the
Rose*.[1] The discussion went to and fro about whether it was
appropriate for people who had been divorced to be allowed
to marry again in church. I felt as if I was in some sort of
parallel universe to the secular one I occupied during the rest
of my life. As if anyone cared! As if the solemn decisions of
the London Diocesan Synod were going to make the slightest
bit of difference to anything. As someone remarked in a rare
moment of sanity, clergy were legally entitled to marry divorced
people already, and weren't likely to stop. If the Church doesn't
even have enough moral authority to control its clergy, what
price the rest of society?

We shouldn't be surprised – we were warned as long ago
as 1983. When Trevor Huddleston preached a sermon to com-
memorate the 150th anniversary of the Oxford Movement, he
made the point quite clearly. He talks about the great issues
confronting society, and the list is one we would still sign up to:
'genetic engineering, the manipulation of human intelligence,
the assault on natural resources', are among the topics he men-
tions. But then he says: 'It would be the height of folly and an
expression of arrogance for the Church – through its leaders
or its synods or its commissions – to imagine it could pronounce

36

with authority (with self-authenticating authority) on *any* of these issues alone. And it is losing, or has lost, its authority precisely by attempting to do so.'[2]

The authority of the Church only really exists when it is regarded as unquestionable. It can expect to be obeyed only so long as the majority of its members accept its authority over them. This can be withdrawn, and will be all the more if the Church fails to respond to the changes going on in society more widely. Falling birth rates across Europe demonstrate that the Roman Catholic Church's teaching on birth control is no longer obeyed even by many who regard themselves as faithful Catholics. And that case also exposes the difficulty for any institution which attempts to make rules that no-one is disposed to obey. For all that the institution may be convinced it's doing the right thing, it merely looks ridiculous. Society at large is no longer hanging on every pronouncement of church leaders to provide a moral lead. The more the Church's leaders behave as if they had that authority, the more they lose the chance to exercise the power that the Church does have: power to use power very differently.

Power is such an attractive thing that even its illusion is worth clinging on to. Better that than admit that the reality has gone. But it has. The churches are no longer powerful institutions, in the traditional sense of being able to guarantee that people will behave in a certain way because the Church so decrees. It is no longer possible to make people think in a certain way, dress in a certain way, avoid particular activities or practise others, merely in order to become a member of your organization. Some may freely choose to – but the game then is already lost. The initiative lies with each individual, not with the Church.

Coercive power has gone – and that is nothing to mourn over. Arguably, Christianity has not shown itself to be naturally adapted to being a religion of the powerful. The New Testament assumes that Christians will be a small and usually persecuted minority – and the appeal of the faith is rooted in a turning away from the norms of culture and society, and an acceptance that you will be hated even by members of your own family. When the Church has had political power, it hasn't usually known how to wield it in a way that later centuries have recognized as particularly Christian. Crusades, Inquisition, defence of slavery, witchcraft trials – we could all write our own list.

The Church needs to learn to lose power gracefully. That is to say, not losing a game, giving up on a struggle or running up the white flag. If the Church is to live a life filled with grace, it can do so in postmodern times only by continually losing – or even better, loosing – power. If the Church, at any level, seems to believe that it can claim authority over anyone, merely through its longevity or supposed spiritual power, it will have that claim mercilessly tested, probably to destruction. It is forced on us by the change of culture – but that enforced change is also the opportunity to engage again with the New Testament pattern of power relations.

It seems that it is only those who have lost power who are able to reflect with any degree of objectivity on its abuse. That is a sad comment on human sinfulness, but at least now the Church is in a position to do what all ex-imperial powers have to do, and re-evaluate the way in which power is distributed. The Church should have the advantage of doing so with the specific example of Jesus' own use of power – which is characterized both by his lack of fear of it, and his willingness to let it go. The danger that the churches will make themselves look ridiculous is overshadowed by the much greater danger that we will fail to grasp the opportunity to preach a much more Jesus-centred message.

As I set out in the last chapter, thinking again about power challenges the fundamental premises around which Catholic Christians have organized themselves. The Catholic tradition has invested hugely in maintaining the authority of the Church and its priesthood, the guarantors of the presence of the Holy

Spirit of God, keeping the faith pure through the generations and teaching with authority what the faith is and how it
should be believed. 'Teaching with authority'[3] was what Jesus
did, and it was remarked on because it was so different from the
approach of other religious teachers. The belief that the Church
needed to do the same has become folded into a particular idea
of what authority is about and how it is exercised. Part of the
uncertainty in the Catholic tradition, it seems to me, is around
the mismatch now obviously existing between the remnants of
the theology of power and the practice of churches in the real
world. Priests may bluster on about some church festival being
'a Holy Day of Obligation', when attendance is compulsory –
but that won't make most people miss their dose of *Dr Who* if
the two happen to conflict.

There might seem to be two equally unpalatable alternatives.
The first is to try to keep up the pretence that the Church as
an institution can just tell people what to do – and that they
will pay attention. If there's no other way of imagining the use
of power, this might seem the only way of remaining faithful
to Jesus. Especially if the other alternative is to give up entirely,
and to re-invent ourselves as a spiritual shopping opportunity in which the customer is always right. But there are more
than two options on the table. Accepting the loss of coercive
power as an opportunity, we have the chance to re-discover a
more authentically Christian approach, and think again about
what it means to follow Jesus, empowered by the Spirit – what
it is we are seeking to hand on and preserve when we teach the
gospel.

So the Church should not merely go along with contemporary society and try to make the best of the majority's view.
When power is set free from formal and coercive structures,
the result is not instantaneous freedom, though it may look a
little like it on the surface. We need some wisdom about the
way power continues to be used and abused in postmodern times.
The Church still needs to speak about power, even though it

may do so without any of its own – but we do need to learn a different language.

The next bit of this chapter is the tough bit – lots of ideas to crunch before I can explain how it all relates to the Church. So I recommend a good cup of coffee and a biscuit before proceeding.

Power in postmodern times: How to abuse it

I'm sitting writing this part of this chapter on the Orcadian island of North Ronaldsay. Where I am staying, there is a wireless network I can tap into, so I can continue to check my emails, the cricket scores and the weather forecast while gazing out of the window at the calm North Sea. Am I more empowered, am I more free? I feel ambiguous about it. I can continue to be in touch – but aren't I supposed to be on holiday? Who's in control of all these systems I'm part of? I wonder if I'm just another addict – 'I could kick email any day', as long as it's not today.

Power in postmodern times is difficult to pin down. Wherever you look, someone else seems to have more power; people feel controlled by the demands of emails, restricted by the call of their mobile phones, even while having the freedom to do all sorts of things that weren't possible just a few years ago. Who have I been freed by – what have I been freed for? Into being available for work anywhere and at any time? Into the availability of constant distraction from whatever is in front of me to do right now? As so often happens, this present reality has been anticipated in science fiction.[4] In a world in which no-one has to work any more, the remaining humans have retreated into complete virtual worlds which give them the chance to select whatever intellectual, physical or emotional situation they want, to develop their gifts and fulfil all possible human potentiality. The only thing they can't do is die. The story is told through the emerging consciousness of one remnant of a human being as despair rises through the achievement, the pleasure, even the fun. But when he attempts to switch off the whole thing, he is prevented by the robot who administers the system, and another universe of exciting possibilities is plugged into his brain. He is free only to have fun.

You can't avoid him if you're going to mention postmodernism and power in the same sentence: Michel Foucault. An extraordinarily creative thinker, one of his main aims was to uncover the mechanisms of power, and the way in which they change. In his analysis of modes of punishment, he charts the transition of authority mechanisms from external, physical coercion into a quasi-therapeutic desire to make us all police ourselves: to make the individual conscience the same as the state's rules. George Orwell's *1984* shows what Foucault describes: Winston Smith, at the end, tells himself, 'He had won the victory over himself. He loved Big Brother.'[5] There is no longer any need for the secret police, for Room 101: he is his own judge and gaoler.

We live in a world in which power is not located as much as it was in institutions with stable and long-lasting identities, or in individuals who have the authority to tell us what to do. 'The new structure of power is dominated by a network geometry, in which power relationships are always specific to a given configuration of actors and institutions.'[6] Manuel Castells[7] gives a sociologist's take – but it's pointing in the same direction. Power is no longer firmly based in specific places and people. You can't make a simple hierarchical map – we're in a 'network society' and power flows through the networks, concentrating on certain nodes at certain times, but always ready to flow elsewhere if the opportunities look better.

One of Foucault's examples makes the point. He describes the horrific death by torture of an attempted regicide in France in 1757.[8] The external apparatus of justice makes it clearly and objectively apparent that the victim's crime is one that undermines the whole nature of the state, embodied in the person of the king. Compare that with one of the most vilified people in twentieth-century Britain, Myra Hindley. I sat in a discussion group one day when the conversation turned to her case. All the other participants were convinced that she should never be released from prison, because, in their view, desiring release meant she wasn't feeling guilty enough. The measure of redemption was her degree of guilt, and the only way to show enough guilt was to realize she should never be released. What they demanded was that Hindley condemn herself as unforgivable.

Contemporary life admits of no such outward and dramatic display of what it means to defy proper authority. Instead we have mechanisms of guilt and remorse, internal policemen who are reinforced by a constant stream of information about what is right and wrong: a message just as strong, but diffused across many different media and percolating into us so that we never consider whether it is our own opinion or that of some external body. A great example of this is shown in the word 'the media'. It used to mean 'the various different bodies which convey information'. Now it's become a singular noun: 'the media' is a way of giving a label (usually pejorative) to the undefinable variety of ways in which we hear about what's going on, what other people think of it, what we might think about it . . . most commonly now, turning completely away from rationality, how people *feel* about . . . whatever it is. But there is no such thing as 'the media'; there is a huge variety of different media, contradicting each other, competing with each other, and together creating an atmosphere of information which no-one feels able to control.

This is all part of what Zygmunt Bauman describes as 'liquid modernity' (and I think is near enough to what most other people call 'postmodernity'). He's not exactly in favour of the whole thing, though he admits that it is popular enough. As he says, 'throughout human history the work of culture consisted in sifting and sedimenting hard kernels of perpetuity out of transient human lives and fleeting human actions, in conjuring up duration out of transience, continuity out of discontinuity, and in transcending thereby the limits imposed by human mortality . . . Demand for this kind of work is nowadays shrinking.'[9] A liquid society has little interest in things of lasting significance as the world is constantly being re-created into new and interesting shapes. Meaning is replaced by enjoyment as a basic principle. The present experience is all there is – the next experience will come along, but it's not necessarily related to what went before. Even desire is in danger of being replaced by mere wishes as the defining 'principle' for a consuming society. Liquid society melts away even further into a gaseous state, with no frameworks or purpose.[10]

It is here that the illusion of freedom can become most dangerous. Without clear external standards against which to measure ourselves or rebel, it is possible so to internalize the unstated standards of behaviour that surround us that we have no moral consciousness at all, of doing either right or wrong. If it feels OK it must be OK. What feels OK is mediated through role models, through the stories we hear, the conversations we have – nothing too authoritarian or definite, and so all the more powerful. We are being manipulated, but no-one admits to being the manipulator. Possibly there really is no-one who feels in control of the system.

If it's difficult to know at any moment where power is being wielded, it's almost impossible then to have a clear sense of progress or achievement. The world of our experience becomes just one set of negotiations after another, and how you did in the last round may have little relationship to your success in the next. In a gaseous world, another parable might be coming true, that of Borges, in his fable of a society in which all social roles are allotted – by lottery – each 60 days.[11] 'Like all the men of Babylon, I have been proconsul; like all, I have been a slave.' But who runs the lottery? Is there a management at all?

If power is always somewhere else, then the most powerful thing about it is its elusiveness. Big institutions that claim power are now no more than targets whose relative powerlessness is demonstrated every day. The new carriers of power keep themselves out of sight, invisible in the network centres of the world – especially the centres of global capitalism, like China, the USA and Western Europe. Image makers, perception consultants and other specialist companies and individuals now create the boundaries of possibility within which governments, corporations and even churches have to work.

If it's increasingly difficult to create a narrative about the world in general, the refuge tends to be the story of the self: 'progress' becomes a personal story of psychological improvement, self-help, etc.[12] And of course that fits quite nicely with the economics of a consumerist society. No need to trouble yourself with the big questions – just focus on whether your own needs are being met.

Let me give you an example. A few years ago I was involved in one of the government's attempts to share power with local people – the New Deal for Communities. Very large sums of money were allocated to areas of deprivation, with the expectation that the structures of power would be controlled by local people. But it wasn't necessarily easy for them, however much they may have been aware that they were kept out of the structures of power heretofore. At one of the early open meetings on the way in which the £50-odd million should be spent, it was suggested that the first call should be on the legal costs of prosecuting the local council for its failure to meet the needs of local people over the years. This was said in all seriousness.

The initial problem was that the lack of power over so many years had created a dynamic of powerlessness, of resentment – the idea of becoming the one who held power was inconceivable except as a weapon of retribution. But merely sharing the money out differently made no difference at all. Holding the cheque book is no longer the key lever. The money follows the power, not the other way round. Power is about the ability to make people do things, and the accurate element of the analysis of despair was that, even with £50+ million, local people would still not be allowed to do whatever they wanted. The regulation, accountability, due process that were required meant that there was, in the end, very little freedom about spending the money. Government could not in fact take the risk of letting local people have real power. Some good things were done, but there wasn't, and there couldn't be, a revolution in the local community's sense of ownership of its own life. Real power was still in 'the system', wherever that may be.

How do you have a revolution in postmodern times? If we aren't converted into our own gaolers, or forced into finding meaning in our own interior worlds exclusively, but continue to want to change the structures of society, we are left with nothing to revolt against. As one blog put it, caricaturing Marx: 'Philosophers merely understand the world. The point is to complain about it.'[13] Customer service departments will apologize endlessly – but that doesn't change policy, or move the locus of power.

The suspicious interpretation of this invisibility of power sees it as some great conspiracy, a new brand of opium for the masses. If religion no longer works in blinding ordinary people to the realities of their oppression, let's give them reality TV instead. One of the great attractions of this interpretation, of course, is that it lets 'the masses' off the hook. It's not their fault that they like fast food, shopping malls and George W. Bush: it's all the fault of sinister executives in converted loft offices. Similar resistance to the new invisible power that seems to have us in its grip is as much behind political movements, especially those of a conservative nationalist trend, as, ironically, it is also behind the protest movements at the other end of the political spectrum.

It also lets us off the hook. If all power is concentrated in the hands of international villains, nothing's our own fault – we have no responsibility. But the problem of power is always more complex than this. Part of the complexity is that we all have power, but no-one has an automatic right to wield it over anyone else. The danger is that we end up in a systemic gridlock; each of us is prepared to wield our own power – as consumer, as voter, even as demonstrator – in order to prevent things happening that affect us, but none of us dares to stick our head above the parapet to attempt to do something new.

Power creates patterns of dependency and expectation that cannot be unravelled simply. If the Church is to be an empowering body, it's not merely a question of standing back and saying 'get on with it' – with the inheritance of generations of power-holding comes the difficult responsibility of enabling oneself to give away, and enabling others to receive and use.

We had to go through all the complexities of this chapter so far, not in order to find a model, but to know where we are. Unless we understand it, we as individuals, and the Church as a body, will all too easily conform to the new paradigm of power as we did to the old one. But in all the slipperiness of thinking about postmodernity, the Church has a huge advantage – a starting point for a radically different language of power: the dynamic of gracefully losing and loosing it. We have a past and a future – a story that resists being folded into the eternal, shallow present of postmodern consumer culture. The example of Jesus is of power being acknowledged and used, without seeking domination. The power of God in Jesus Christ is perhaps not seen in that greatest miracle: to have absolute power without being corrupted by it at all.

Thinking theologically about power

The Church, unless we find a new way forward, is pretty much stuck. We no longer have any real coercive power to wield, and we certainly aren't part of the slippery network of power as it is deployed in postmodern societies. And, as we have seen, neither option is much good as a reflection of the gospel of Jesus in any case. So let's return to the basics, and think about how we might use power as the Church of Jesus Christ.

God is all-powerful – that's one of the things you say about God in order to check you're talking of the same sort of God as other people are talking of. God is not one god, slugging it out with a lot of other divinities; God is the only creator of all that is or will be. Omnipotence is the word. Jesus, on the other hand, wasn't powerful at all, at least not in the way God is powerful. Jesus refused the opportunity to take the Jewish people in hand and lead them to glory against the Romans; he wasn't interested even in saving his own life. Yet the records about him also speak of his power over the elements, his ability to restore life, the authority of his teaching, his most extraordinary power to enable human beings to leave their lives of sin and death and find new hope in following him – even if they weren't exactly sure why.

I'd like to suggest that part of the Church's problem with power – its theological problem, as opposed to the ordinary problems of being sinful human beings – is that we've tended to start with the divine omnipotence as our image of power, rather than Jesus' more complex approach to it. I suppose it was inevitable. The divine omnipotence has been the model to which human rulers have aspired through the ages, usually eventually to their own cost. It appears in the New Testament, sure enough, but always in the context of eschatology: that is, reflection on the heavenly realities that lie beyond this world, the realities that will be revealed at the end of time. Of course there have always been protest movements, living a different vision of the Christian calling – let's just mention St Francis as an example among many others – but the dominant paradigm remained the one of power and control.

In the pursuit of power, the Church has shown a great ability to transpose the heavenly vision into earthly reality – or try to, at least. The vision of God's throne room in Revelation chapter 4 is seen in this way by Stephen Moore in his wonderful book *God's Gym*.[14] For Moore, it is a profoundly unhealthy vision of God that develops in Revelation, an 'ideology . . . which relies on a combination of pseudo-religious attitudes and the brutal use of power for getting and keeping power'.[15] Of course he is right in suggesting that Revelation takes the language and imagery of emperor worship and translates it into the vision of God's glory. But this pure power is pure, because it is envisioned in the eschatological end time, when God is all in all; it is power that does not disempower. And it is quite the opposite from the power exercised by Jesus, which is the model for the Church. This is not Foucauldian self-policing, because there is in fact no difference between the outer and the inner desire; God's will for creation is its own perfected desire.

But we're not there yet. If the Church claims to have the full and perfect vision of what everyone needs, then the Inquisition is the only result, because people will keep on disagreeing. So if the eschatological vision is translated into a programme for the life of the Church, and the Church's claims about what it can do and what it should be, then Moore's quite right. But Revelation 4 and similar passages sit outside time, in the eschaton, the end, when the world is being wound up. The vision in Revelation 4 is quite explicitly not of how things are in this world, but a revelation of the heavenly reality. It's not meant to be a groundplan for the organization of the Church.

God's omnipotence is literally incomprehensible: we can't get our heads around it. It's something we have to affirm as a pointer towards what we mean by the word 'God', but in our world we can't really know what it means. All we're doing is excluding some things we know we *don't* mean when talking about God. The one we do know is Jesus, the one in whom God became flesh and blood, the one in whom God operated as an actor within this world. It's Jesus' example we should be following when we look at the way the Church uses power.

But there's still a problem – a big one. One of the main targets of Jacques Derrida's philosophical work was what he called 'logocentrism', by which he meant all the (in his view, vain) attempts to find a philosophical ground from which everything else could start – a 'logos', *word*, which is the foundation and origin of all other ways of thinking. For Derrida, whatever explanation we seek to start from, we are always already bound up in the network of human thought, which is constructed by our language. There are no words that do not get their meaning from the network of other words, a meaning potentially infinite, and quite uncontrollable. Meaning leaks out of our efforts to pipe it neatly through sequences of language. It's not that there is no truth, but that there is no philosophical place in which one could stand and definitively assess all other truth claims. Wherever one takes one's (philosophical) stand, one is already dependent on a train of argument, on a specific tradition. You can't get outside it.

Postmodernity too is defined by a suspicion of claims to absolute truth. That's why traditional sources of authority are always under threat. And what can be more logocentric than a religion that describes its main figure as the *Logos*, the Word with a capital W? Obvious as it might seem, the connection is completely wrong. The logocentrism attacked by Derrida and suspected more generally in postmodern times is quite different from the person of Jesus Christ.

Jesus is the Word, though – famously so in the prologue of John's Gospel, the Word which was from the beginning, the very source and origin which I have argued cannot exist in this world. So am I denying the nature of God in my efforts to remake our thinking about power? I hope not; and I think the description of Jesus as the Word is consistent with what I have been trying to depict in the paradox of the God who is beyond this world, and yet enters it without seeking to control. One of the challenges of Christian theology has always been to try to hold together the divine and the human in Christ, without losing or diminishing either. Jesus is both the eternal Word of God, and also empties himself into the man from Nazareth. He is on both the outside and the inside of our world: he holds together the fact that God is not divided.

It's claiming to be the end point, to set oneself up as the arbiter and guarantor of truth, that places oneself outside the contingencies of the world of which we're part. It's just not something we can authentically claim, because there is no place outside the world from which the claim can be made. 'God' is the word we use to point towards the one whom we experience as being outside of all of this: the source and origin in which all things hang together. But because we're on the inside of the world's complexities, we cannot claim to know the essence of God. We can't understand God, though God knows us through and through. What we can do, in Christ and through his Spirit, is to have a relationship of love and trust. And that is what Jesus did too: he pointed by his own self beyond his own self. He and the Father are one: but he does nothing that does not come from his Father. Jesus is the *Logos* which continually refers and defers to the other persons of the Trinity. Most of all, he is a person, not a philosophical principle. As a man with his fellow human beings, he lived a life which served others, in which power flowed out from him into those around him.

Jesus and power

Jesus wasn't a great one for institutions. I'm pretty sure that institutions as such are a demonstration of the fallen nature of humanity. We can't do without them, but we can't do very well with them either. Institutions are capable of banal evil never intended by any of the individuals who serve them. We must always live in tension with the institutions we cannot do without. But I'm not sure Jesus would really have been keen on the 'network society' and the 'space of flows' either. Wherever power is centralized, or diverted away from those on the margins, the dynamic in play is probably not one of which he would wish to be part.

Jesus was not powerless; he was full of power for others. The power that flowed through him was continually dispersed, given away, eternally diffused. Jesus was full of power, but never powerful, because his power was never used to dominate or to control. It flowed out from him, but he never allowed it to flow back the other way. So when the people came to make him king – the ultimate recognition of power – he withdrew from them: in other words, he ran away. This is all of a piece with the interpretation of the Gospels I outlined in the last chapter; it's the working out of God's setting aside the right to dictate to human beings, and instead entering the world by our side and on our side. The God who empties Godself in the incarnation continues that self-emptying in the life of Jesus – and that is what we should model in the life of the Church.

But where does this power come from that is eternally given away? How is it that it doesn't just drain Jesus dry? And even if he could do it, what price the rest of us? If we were to try living like this, what guarantee would we have that it would work? That's the difficult bit: we have no other guarantee than Jesus did, that is, the promise of God's Holy Spirit. The Spirit blows where it wills and you can't control it. And that's exactly the point.

A relationship of true love is not a relationship of control: power is not deployed within it to dominate. That's the ideal to which all of us in long-term loving relationships fail to live up. That's the relationship Jesus had perfectly with his Father, and that's the route through which power flowed through him into the world. Jesus was not in control, he was not the centre – so he would always point back to his Father through whom he received everything. He both knows the Father intimately, and yet does not presume to use that knowledge as power.

Power in the Church

This all might seem very trendy. But though this isn't the way I might phrase it, I think the address given by K. E. Kirk to the 1933 Anglo-Catholic Congress is heading in the same direction: 'We shall do no good with easy truisms or trite platitudes or unintelligent repetitions of age-old *formulas*. The only authority which men will respect . . . is an authority which, however firmly it bases itself upon the proved truths of the past, is vivacious enough to bring them into vital contact with the ever-changing moods of the present.'[16]

The story of Jesus is not one that can be corralled within the life of Jesus: because it is also the story of God, it breaks every boundary that we can construct for it. Before history Jesus is there; after history Jesus rises from the dead. The Christian story always has more to say; it gives itself into other stories, but is never exhausted. The story of the gospel is one that is always telling itself again, in new and surprising and even worrying ways. The story of Jesus begins with his story as a Jewish man in Palestine, but that story is continually sowing new seeds in new places.

The stories aren't all identical, even from the beginning. The Gospels do not tell exactly the same story, though they all point towards the same person. Even from the origin of the Church, there are too many stories to tell of Jesus to fit them all into one narrative: his truth is bigger than our words, however encyclopaedic we try to be. Perhaps it is in the very paradox that our stories of God do not quite marry up that we create the fault line through which God who is beyond the world can enter the world without destroying it by the absoluteness of his presence. In any case, we as the Church must continually re-tell the story, while knowing that we are leaving out so much else that could be said.

Even to proclaim a fixed and absolute humility and renunciation of power is to claim too much. Power used in the way Jesus showed us always starts by subverting all claims to domination, and re-asserting the contingency of power as emanating from relationships of love. The violence of the Kingdom is a violence against all claims to holding power – all claims to 'logocentrism': against claims to have the central 'word' which interprets all others.

So I am suggesting that, in a renewed Christian theology, the Church's loss of power and the insights of contemporary philosophy together give us the chance to embrace a view of power as loving gift: a gift given only to be given away, with no return sought or desired. Jesus gave his own life without reserve, in order to give life to others: he held open a doorway through which God's power could flow into and through the world.

And how do we do the same? Through the gift of God's Holy Spirit, by which the same power is at work in us. We can't control the Spirit – if anything, it's the other way round. But if we entrust ourselves to the wind of the Spirit, the promise is that we will have the same gift that Jesus did. The Church has found it very difficult to know what to do with this, but that's the challenge that continually confronts us.

What would it look like for the Church to live like that? We'd still need to get things done, and we'd still want to choose people who were able to fulfil the roles they were given. The Church couldn't become an anarchist commune and continue to be church. But that is a sort of resort to the myth of powerlessness. Each of us has our own power – of personality, of education, of connectedness to networks. As the priest of a parish, I'm only too aware that the real power is not held by me – nor by any other individual. The real power of the community is that which is forged by the relationships of the whole body, for good or bad. The impossible revolution, which is the only hope for the Church to find a way of being an institution with power in postmodern times, is the turning around of our power so that it is used for others and not for ourselves. This is not a new teaching, but it is still one that the Church has not managed to grasp in many of its structures and patterns of behaving.

4

Churches and their priests

The presence of what is alien, pagan, unholy, unclean at the heart of the church is essential to its nature. When the church finds what is unholy, then it must say 'For this too Christ died' ... In such moments the Church too must die, must swallow its pride, give up the boundary which it thought defined its existence, and discover a new and larger vocation. And that new vocation will itself be defined by a new boundary which in time the Church will also have to transcend.[1]

A couple of years after I was ordained, I attended a large church gathering, of people from across many dioceses. Since it was out of the parish where I was serving, and I wasn't there in an official capacity, I went in casual clothes. Those who know me will realize this is really quite casual: it was a hot summer, so T-shirt, shorts and sandals was about it. Suddenly I was invisible, as I hadn't been for two years. As far as everyone there was concerned, I was just half of a young couple with a baby. I didn't matter – and in particular, I didn't matter to the other clergy there, all properly dressed in clerical collars. Had I been wearing my uniform, people (not just other clergy) would have wanted to get to know me, find out who I was and where I was from, but I was suddenly back in the throng of the uninteresting laity – God's ordinary people.

If the Church is to become anything like what I talked about in the last chapter, that sort of thing has got to stop. We all know (well, most of us know) that those who are called to leadership, and particularly to ordained ministry, are no more important in the eyes of God than anyone else. In which case, one might think, the same should go for the life of the Church. But hierarchy (which literally means 'the rule of the priests') seems to be one of the eternal temptations of human beings, and it's one that Catholics have appropriated so completely we have for years called it a virtue.

In 1968 Faith Press, practically an official voice of Anglo-Catholicism, published *No Priest, No Church*, a broadside against the proposal at that time for union between the Anglican and Methodist Churches in England. The author, F. H. Mountney MA, trawls through church tradition in order to find as much evidence as possible for affirming that the Church of England by its tradition holds to (Roman) Catholic views of the ordained ministry. He is particularly horrified by the idea that the foreign doctrine of the Priesthood of All Believers (his capitals, which I will not continue to use) should be brought into the Church of England. Among his supporters he quotes the great Anglo-Catholic scholar, Eric Mascall: 'The ministry as it is conceived in Catholic theology . . . exists indeed not apart from the Church but IN the Church and FOR the Church . . . But it does not come FROM the Church, but FROM Christ, who is the Church's head.'[2] Of course, if that is the case then the ordained ministry are in a separate category from the rest of the people of God, and a certain view of church life and organization necessarily follows on. Hierarchy is doctrinally unavoidable – despite the rather obvious words of Jesus about the first being last, and whoever would be a leader needing to be the slave of everyone else.

But that's not the only Catholic voice. In the second edition of *The Christian Priest Today*, in 1985, Michael Ramsey included an essay entitled 'Priesthood: Jesus and the people of God' in which he sets out a rather different vision. Returning to scriptural sources, he says, 'Hebrews and 1 Peter tell of the priesthood of Christ and the priesthood of the Church. The ordained ministry serves both, and indeed will have authority from both . . . So today the ordained ministry is called to reflect the priesthood of Christ and to serve the priesthood of the people of God, and to be one of the means of grace whereby God enables the Church to be the Church.'[3]

In Ramsey's words, the opportunity opens up for us to find the sort of authentically Catholic view of the priesthood that I was looking for in chapter 2, which finds its life not in claiming authoritarian power over against the rest of God's people, but in living out the self-giving power of Christ with and for the Church and in service to the world. Priesthood, then, can only be properly thought about in relation to the life of the whole Church, but it's not reducible to the life of the Church – priests aren't just people who are paid to do what all Christians are called to do. In chapter 2, I quoted from Charles Gore these words about the Church's ministry: 'the apostolic ministry, which all must accept, instituted by Christ in the persons of the Twelve and continued in the succession of the bishops down the ages, linking the different churches together by the fellowship of the bishops throughout the world and binding the succession of generations to the apostolic original'. The question for me is whether we can see that succession, not as a spiritual police force, but as the passing on of a Tradition which is not repeated, but renewed, in each age.[4]

Passing the parcel

So how can an authentically Catholic approach to faith manifest itself in a Church which uses power differently, which has a renewed vision of priesthood? I think we've got the resources now, from the path we've walked through the last few chapters, to sketch out something which, though very different from Catholic traditional practice, grows authentically out of Catholic tradition. But where to start? Priesthood and Church serve each other reciprocally. From a traditional perspective, Christ first calls the apostles (from whom the ordained ministry derives, in theory). Another way of looking at the apostles is as just the first followers of Christ – the first lay people of the Church. How could one disentangle those strands from what we have in the New Testament? But one principle we do have, which is that the first shall be last. As a priest, used to being among 'the first' in the Church's organizational life, I think we should start with the Church, the whole people of God.

Liquid Church?

Having made reference to Bauman's *Liquid Modernity*, the natural place to start perhaps for thinking about the Church in a postmodern age is Pete Ward's book, *Liquid Church*.[5] He sees the Church primarily as formed by networks – dynamic, informal, un-institutional modes of being, which he sees also as a biblical model: he claims that Paul in I Corinthians is setting up the small, networked group as his model for the Church.

Ward wants to strengthen the concept of 'church' so that 'in church' becomes more like 'in Christ' – 'church' no longer refers to buildings and places, but directly to the community of faith. In doing so, he is (quite reasonably) following through one of the basic evangelical concepts with which Catholics have trouble. For him, 'church' does not imply any particular form of church order – its importance theologically is to be the best possible gathering place (not necessarily in one physical space) for the body of individuals who have responded to Christ in discipleship. It's a container only, so what shape it might take is determined pretty much on pragmatic grounds: what sort of organization will bring most people into a relationship with Jesus and will enable them to live a life of faith within the community of believers?

In order to re-establish contact at this point with those of you reading this and wondering what planet I'm living on, I say again that this comes out of my experience in university chaplaincy and inner urban parish ministry in London. Even in that context, there's still plenty of what we might, following Ward, describe as 'solid church' still going on. Ordinary parish life is still alive and strong, as is traditional liturgy. In my present post I have become, somewhat to my own surprise, a bit of an expert in the Book of Common Prayer. You don't get much more traditional than a liturgy that hasn't changed substantially since 1662, but I have seen people come to faith through using it in worship. I don't think that will change: traditional forms of liturgy will I think come to life again within a postmodern context, but no longer as forms of nostalgia; they won't have wistful memories attached. But enough digressing; the point is that traditional and postmodern – solid and liquid – forms of church will continue to exist, and in many places solid church is the overwhelming norm. But eventually, I believe, the changes that go under the banner of postmodernity will become the norm. The greatest danger is that the Church's priests will so collude with the old model, actively supporting and sustaining it within their congregations, that a chasm will open up between the attitudes of those who attend church and the wider community of which they are part – a chasm of misunderstanding that will make it almost impossible for anyone new to join the church community.

A liquid church for a liquid society – sounds ideal, a perfect match. But Ward doesn't appear to notice that Bauman sees the liquid society not as a utopia, but as the opposite – a dystopia. A solid society is one that 'fixes space and binds time', and those are vital functions because they provide us with the building blocks for creating human meaning. The meaningless succession of present moments gives nothing to hold on to but the pleasure of each moment; it is the philosophy of daily hedonism. Not that time and space disappear; but if there is no basis on which to think and create our past, present and future, we are in the grip of forces we do not recognize or understand. As John Maynard Keynes put it in another context: 'Practical men, who believe themselves to be quite exempt from any intellectual influences, are usually the slaves of some defunct economist.'[6] When it comes to faith, it can be even more frightening. The Christian tradition is only too aware of the propensity of the human heart to sin, and the complete absence of 'solid' frameworks leaves all too much space for human sinfulness to flourish.

Coming from a Catholic perspective, my anxiety is that an overly pragmatic welcome of a 'liquid' way of being church may unwittingly open the door to forces that can overwhelm the Church entirely. A liquid church in a liquid society may merely become yet another momentary lifestyle choice. I haven't yet had recourse to another of my main inspirations in understanding society, but here he comes: Terry Pratchett. His fantasy books aren't just good fun – they're also great satire, illuminating some uncomfortable corners of human ways of being. In *Making Money*,[7] he introduces a new twist on the fashion of the book club.

'god of the month'

A group of respectable middle-aged ladies, in Pratchett's alternative world, choose a different god each month, and experiment with worshipping him / her / it, and then meet to discuss their experiences. Worship is not even so much a matter of self-fulfilment, as a way of passing the time for people whose lives are otherwise slightly boring. If only that were as distant from our own society as we would like to imagine.

In a postmodern liquid society, the Church needs to know how to challenge wrongdoing – in the wider world or in its own members. It needs to have a history, a story, a memory and a hope: to be placed in space and time. And it needs to do all of this without using models of thought and practice that are rooted in a framework of society that is now passing. The Church needs to know how to speak truth confidently in a non-foundational age. It needs to be something other than the traditional solid institution – Ward's quite right about that – but it also needs to be other than a liquid church in a liquid society. From a Catholic perspective, the truth that the Church proclaims needs to be embodied in its collective life, even in postmodern times.

'God lets himself be pushed out of the world onto the cross.'[8] It is this story we tell, one of a Jesus who both is and is not in this world – a Jesus who does not demand our attention but invites it. After the resurrection, his presence in the Church through the Spirit continues this elusiveness. The Spirit blows where it wills: it can't be controlled. Jesus' continued presence in the Church is both comforting and unsettling. In the Church, Jesus is here; but no-one can point to where exactly he is, unless we point towards the Blessed Sacrament – or each other. Wherever it is that he is, there is always something else more visibly there as well: an ordinary human being, or the physical elements of bread and wine. We cannot remove the physical and earthly reality and have something left that we can point to and say, 'there's Jesus'. The paradox is that we can be completely confident of Christ's presence, but never able to locate him precisely and without remainder.

How is it possible to avoid claiming truth in a way that is really a claim to power? Well, it all depends on what sort of truth you're after. 'The truth is out there' – yes, the Church claims that in God we meet the ultimate Truth, the one in whom all other truths find their truthfulness. But, if the Church can learn humility about its own ownership of that claim, about defining its meaning and contents, there may be a way forward. I want to argue that the key truth of Christian faith is not a set of doctrines, but an encounter – with Christ who is the Truth, Way and Life. Truth is inter-personal, it is found in relationship. In that sense of truth there is a possible connection with, as well as a challenge to, the truth sought in the 'How do you feel?' questions now endemic in news broadcasts. It's a question that tries to get beyond ideas and thoughts, and to create a meeting with what is perceived to be the authentic heart of the interviewee, that person's feelings. We offer such a meeting, but one that doesn't merely provide an interesting voyeur's view. The meeting with Christ is one that puts our whole life in question and, if we respond seriously, makes us change direction: repent.

But you can't dictate encounters. During my (rather brief) charismatic phase, long ago, I found myself continually meeting people who were overwhelmingly keen that we should all experience the baptism of the Holy Spirit. The problem was that if you didn't experience it their way, it probably wasn't genuine. Relationship isn't like that; it isn't the same for everyone. To preach that Truth doesn't lead to everyone responding in the way we might like. So how do we avoid creating a designer religion – I'll believe whatever I fancy and call it Christianity?

Truth is inter-personal – it is shared, and built up in community. Each of us encounters the truth of Christ in our own way, but that's not the end of the story. The Church is the body in which truth is shared, explored, and made manifest. The encounter with Christ is individual, but never individualistic: that is one of the continuing claims with which the Church must challenge the trends of society. To quote him again, Michael Ramsey wrote: 'Individualism has no place in Christianity, and Christianity, verily, means its extinction.'[9] So the individual is not the sole point of authority in relation to his or her own life, which is the end of individual*ism*.

Not the sole point of authority, but not completely submissive either – except to God. The Church cannot convincingly claim to have such a direct sense of the will of God that it can try to be a coercive authority. Power which is anti-individualistic, without being rigid and authoritarian – that is, power which can carry authority in 'the ever-changing moods of the present'[10] – that's what we're after. The theological principle that needs to be recovered is that of the *consensus fidelium*. Usually this is translated as 'the consent of the people' – the Church's agreement to the doctrines handed down from on high – and this appears to be how it is mostly understood on its home ground in the Roman Catholic Church. It could also be used as a way of describing the collective discernment of the body of Christ, and translated, somewhat freely, as 'the common sense of God's people'. One Christian body that is famous for its approach to business is the Society of Friends, the Quakers. Here is a description of the conduct of a meeting for business:

> A meeting starts with a period of quiet worship. The clerk then opens the business part of the meeting. As in a secular meeting, someone presents an item, and answers questions of clarification. But rather than debating the matter, the gathering then tries to discern, in an atmosphere of worship, what love requires of us. Spoken contributions are offered as ministry and are wrapped in silence. If things seem to be getting heated, the clerk or another Friend may ask for a period of silence. A touch of humour often helps the process. No vote is taken, as we are not trying to reach consensus or establish the will of the majority, but to work in harmony with the Spirit. This approach can be very liberating, because it ensures that minority views are not dismissed or suppressed. A minute is drafted by the clerk and presented to the meeting; it is for all those present to agree the record of their deliberations.[11]

It's much more difficult, perhaps, when you have professional ministry, liturgies, creeds. Structures and systems naturally become gathering places for coercive power. But that's why the calling is also so urgent to find ways of holding them lightly, so that power flows outwards, is given away. By living the example of Jesus, the Church has the opportunity to discover that power is not a zero-sum game: it's not a question that if I give some away to you, you've got more and I've got less. It can equally be that we both have more: power can multiply. If individuals within a church find themselves enabled to do things they couldn't do before, that doesn't have to be at the expense of others – so long as the leadership has created a climate in which power is a virtuous and not a vicious circle. The radical equality of all that the Quakers attempt to practise can also be the root of a Church that continues to celebrate the sacraments, and to honour its priesthood (an odd thought, perhaps, but it's what 'reverend' means).

Maybe it would help to recognize that the Church is not the Kingdom of heaven – not that anyone, when confronted with it explicitly, is likely to make the mistake. The Church maybe is the republic of God's people on earth, a republic awaiting its final transformation into the perfect Kingdom. But in the meantime we know that none of us has royal rights; we must therefore continually seek to negotiate our perceptions of the Truth whom we meet through the patient paths of negotiation and reconciliation.

As I write this part of the book, I have been a member of the Church of England's General Synod (a sort of twice-a-year Parliament) for three years. I find each meeting profoundly unsettling, because there seems an unresolved tension in the air. We are mostly elected, and mostly because we represent one or other of the different interest groups in the Church: some of us are for, some against women's priestly ministry; some are evangelicals, some Catholics, and so on. But we are also aware that we come together all as Christian people who have in common our deepest beliefs and hopes. I feel as if we oscillate between those two poles, never able to find a stable position. Maybe if we were to think of ourselves as negotiators, we might get somewhere. In a negotiation, all parties are upfront about having different priorities and goals, but the very process of entering negotiation is (or at least is meant to be) a sign of good faith in seeking common ground. Good negotiation requires, if anything else is to happen at all, a level of trust. It also implies the ending of absolutist positions, which are rooted, in church settings, in a conviction of knowing exactly what God wants.

It is that ending of absolutisms, and even more importantly the building of trust, which will need to be at the core of church life in a postmodern age. We are all acutely sensitive to hidden agendas and ulterior motives, because we are trained to look for them everywhere. Growing in a culture of suspicion, trust is a fragile plant. At every level of the Church's life, it will have to be fostered through genuine commitment to mutuality, and protected by processes that make it difficult for deceit to be imputed. How that works out in practice will have to be different in different places, and it would be far too boring to try to describe it here. In any case, it's the living principle that alone could make this sort of Church live, not any number of plans or blueprints.

But with all this participation, even if you do manage to make a decision, how can you guarantee to keep the Church within the historic, Catholic faith? How does the Church retain the boundaries it must have if it is to have any distinct identity? Does it still have any authority at all? I believe it can still have all these things, though without the power to enforce them. Setting aside the power of enforcement in fact may be the only way to continue to exist as a body at all, in the long term. But it is risky: it's about taking the risk that relationships of trust, mutuality and inclusion are strong enough to reinforce unity and coherence. As I write, it seems as if the churches of the Anglican Communion are shying away from the challenge, and many are looking instead for a large-scale enforcement operation in order to maintain orthodoxy. Interestingly, though, it also seems that some are ready to trust, to delay, to work through building up deeper relationships of mutual care. Whether or not the Anglican Communion has gone one way or another by the time you read this, the way of trust is still the way to go.

Some of you may think I'm just not being realistic, so let me tell you a story about money, from my own experience. All the churches in the deanery where I was working had to make their contribution to the diocesan pot, the Common Fund. Some years previously, the churches had abandoned the practice of calculating a certain amount of money that each was supposed to be able to afford, and then demanding it. Instead, the costs of ministry were talked about collectively, and each church was asked to contribute as generously as it could. And because it was founded on relationships of trust, the amount of money given went up. Even more remarkably, when one parish was in really difficult circumstances, the rest of the deanery picked up its contribution for a year. Of course, when that parish's finances recovered, it made a generous contribution – the virtuous cycle was in place. If it can happen with money, it can happen with anything.

A church that instated mutual trust – let's be honest, mutual love – in its administrative frameworks would be a wonder to behold. That church would have something for postmodern times – something to give that is dying elsewhere. It would be that rarest of things – a community that is non-coercive, and doesn't dump its anxieties on those outside it. Bauman thinks it is impossible: 'An inclusive community would be a contradiction in terms.'[12] If it is possible, it is only through the work of the Holy Spirit.

This could be a church that creates in the surface present of the postmodern world a story that makes sense of the present in relation to the past – to a tradition that informs, resources and founds the present, but does not control it; and to the future – a future of hope. In such a setting, Ward's ambition might be realized, that the Church's life might be characterized by 'the pursuit of the holy';[13] the Church might foment desire for God, not merely meet needs for reassurance.

Bauman can see little hope for the future. Even the idea of pilgrimage is given a dystopian (because this-worldly) interpretation.[14] But a community on a pilgrimage towards a real utopia (a contradiction in terms, since 'utopia' means 'nowhere' – the unimaginable place where God reigns) – that might provide a place and a framework within which many would want to re-tell their own stories of themselves, and weave themselves into a greater story. It's a metanarrative, yes, but one in which the meanings are found through encounter and negotiation, an open-ended narrative in which the characters are also the authors. A very ancient, postmodern story.

Priests for God's people

The role of the priest finds itself in relation to the community. That is what I discovered as a member of Holy Joe's. It is by the community that priests are called; it is in part from the community that they take what authority they are given. But the Christian community does something else. It recognizes in those it calls to be priests that they are also called to represent in a special way the ministry of Jesus. Once ordained, priests are not merely lay people with clerical collars; something else is given in ordination. It was once difficult to find clergy, as they were likely to be especially persecuted; we may perhaps be entering another similar time, when those who offer themselves for any public role are automatically targets. For those called to ordination, a ministry of humility may be non-optional.

But however painful it may be for the ordained, it is none-theless good for the Church that the same changes that are destroying the Church as a power-full organization have also diminished the role of the priesthood, and not only because priests are now working in a smaller and less influential organ-ization. We have suffered – if that is the word – from the same loss of respect as has afflicted other professions as well. Some of us, though, have suffered from it more than others. Those in the Catholic tradition are left particularly bereft when the model of priesthood and ministry we have been working with no longer seems to work. That's for good reasons: we're not purely pragmatic about these things; they represent and embody something profound about the sacramental nature of our ministry and of the Church. We can't just change the way we work as a pragmatic response to the way culture has changed – as most evangelicals can, because the way in which the Church is ordered is not in the same way at the heart of their understanding of faith.

I was talking to a friend who had been appointed to a very large parish, in the Catholic tradition. He wisely decided to ask some colleagues in similar-size parishes about how they approached their roles. Most of them (the way the Church is at the moment) were evangelicals. The thing that struck him (according to my recollection of our conversation) was that there was no problem for these clergy in adopting a role in relation to their congregations that was quasi-episcopal: that is to say, they saw their responsibilities in terms of overall governance of the parish's life, in terms of ensuring the provision of pastoral care and in terms of resourcing the leadership team. They were not concerned about the fact that they personally didn't go out visiting the sick very often, still less spend time at the retired ladies' tea meeting.

For most priests in the Catholic tradition, there is a huge amount invested in exactly those things. Along with the regular and public celebration of the sacraments, the day-to-day practice of those pastoral activities is seen not as a particular manifestation of priesthood, but the very heart of it. It's a sure way to raise your status with other clergy – to casually mention that you took the last rites to a dying parishioner, which made you late for the meeting. Planning an evangelistic course or meeting with your house group leaders wouldn't have the same cachet.

Most priests are not (unless things change even more radically than I expect) going to be leading churches with hundreds of members, and the resources to employ their own staff. But we will all be faced with the same challenge: what is essential to the practice of priesthood in postmodern society, and what is just the model we've inherited?

Except not everywhere – and this is one of the great difficulties for the institutional Church. Churches are notoriously
conservative institutions, and the continued existence and even
occasional flourishing of 'solid church' is one of the great temptations facing the clergy. It tempts me; as I said earlier, there's
a lot that's very 'solid', and healthily so, where I work now. If
there is anywhere in contemporary society where professionals
can still plausibly think of themselves as having an uncon-
tested public role, it is within many church communities and
organizations. Tradition gives stability to the role of the priest
within the community of faith that it doesn't have outside –
and that creates one of the temptations facing priests today.
That is, to burrow further and deeper into the comfort zone
in which roles are stable and status is (relatively) assured. I'm
sure it won't work. Change will happen more slowly in some
places than in others, but it will come.

So a retreat into the laager is still possible – and quite
tempting, especially when it seems to offer some continued reassurance in continuing to work in the traditional ways – but it
is doomed in the medium term. It's this that the much-disparaged
work in 'new ways of being church' is trying to point out. It's
not about re-packaging, just a marketing ploy – it's about trying
to find practical ways of responding to a new society.[15] But for
many Catholics, it doesn't scratch where they itch – it doesn't
answer the theological problem of what a priest is called to be
in this new context. There's no point in just saying the old is
dead if there's no resurrection to point to as well. Ironically –
as throughout this book – I believe that, re-appropriated and
re-understood, it is a Catholic understanding of priesthood
that has more to offer than any other to a society in need of
spiritual guidance.

The last thing priests should be doing – the last thing they
are needed for now – is to try to become something other
than their calling. The world already has plenty of impre-
sarios, managers, social activists, fund-raisers, etc. Postmodern

society is used to people who seek to persuade, influence and inform. In a world of communications and information, the good news is not communicated most forcefully by joining the marketplace in which the jaded palate of the consuming public flits increasingly quickly from one pleasure to another. Priests need to be able to listen before they speak, to remember the art of silence, to rejoice in their sacramentality – to be people who stand for something different, not just a product. But that too is not the same as fulfilling a certain set of roles, performing a certain repertoire of actions. Being a priest in the Catholic tradition is more difficult than it was, because it's not about what you do – it's the way that you do it.

What is the role of the priest when public figures are no longer seen as public, but instead as private figures who claim to have something to give everyone else? I think it is that which is at the heart of the contradiction facing the clergy today. It's not merely because of suspicion concerning child abuse scandals and so on; it's not just because all authority claims are instantly regarded as suspicious and needing to be tested to destruction. The very idea of anyone having a role as a public person is now contested; priests like everyone else are evaluated not by how well they fulfil a set role, but by their perceived personal authenticity in doing what they do. So it is their private lives that really matter – the role itself no longer carries anything. The leader has no authority except his or her own personality and charisma.

It's pretty difficult for newly ordained clergy; suddenly they're thrust into a position that no longer carries with it an assumed role, a recognized place. It's very unlike my experience as a newly ordained curate in Carlisle in 1988. I found myself (aged 27) suddenly treated as someone who knew the answers – in my little field at least. Never having been one to betray my lack of confidence, I pretended I did, but fortunately we all survived. Those with whom I have worked more recently, entering ordination, have a much trickier time; one (female) colleague has been asked several times 'Are you real?'

But there is a deep tradition in reflection on ordination which emphasizes this very aspect – albeit in very different language. The priest is 'marked'; something changes through the act of ordination. It's language that has been very unfashionable, a claim we have fought shy of as we have become more conscious of our fallibility – our own, and that of our fellow priests, as scandals have proliferated. It is a more profound and significant understanding, though, of the calling of a priest than the pastoral practices we have got used to clothing it in.

Bauman remarks that 'leadership has been replaced by the spectacle'.[16] For him this is unequivocally negative, but spectacle is what priests do: we let ourselves be looked at. The Church needs priests who are not afraid to be seen, counter-cultural and odd as that may be. If we are 'marked' by God, let that be what we display to the world. Unlike counsellors, psychotherapists and others who offer the various forms of therapy now available, we do not just work on our own, in private consultations, seeing people one at a time. Our work is still public, because it is to enable people to find themselves, not as self-fulfilled independent beings, but as mutually fulfilling interdependent children of God: the Church is meant to be the place where that happens. No wonder vocations are fewer among young people in the Catholic tradition: maybe they've worked out very accurately the commitment demanded of them if they put themselves forward for ordination. The calling to take on a public role, when there is no societal consensus as to what it might be, to continue to witness to the indispensability of other people in a privatized and individualized age – it's no small vocation. To want to be a priest must be either a sign of significant weirdness, or the call of God.

Digging deeper into tradition

The priestly calling is not less than it has been; it is more. The Church now needs priests who will enable it to embody its calling, and who will demonstrate that calling to the world: the calling to live 'on the borders of the holy',[17] to make the things of the unknowable God known, especially through the ministry of the sacraments. The Church's priests need to be all the more rooted in the sacraments as they become strange to the society of which we are part. It is that very strangeness that is their power. They need to be those who enable the Church to become a community pursuing holiness.

Some years ago I conducted a retreat for those preparing for priesthood. This is part of what I had to say:

> Our calling is not to be the ones who are holier than the rest, nor to control the flow of holiness through word and sacrament, but to witness to the generous love of God offering holiness in the most unholy of situations, and to and through the most unlikely of people, even ourselves.
>
> So what does it mean for us to be called to holiness? It doesn't mean that a certain button gets pressed when the bishop's hands alight on your head, and you switch from secular to sacred. It doesn't mean you need to satisfy yourself that you've reached a certain level of virtue before you can celebrate the eucharist. It is a calling not to a state of being but to a journey. One of the most challenging ways in which it is expressed is through the commitment in the covenant service of the Methodist Church, in which the congregation says together:

> > I am no longer my own but yours.
> > Your will, not mine, be done in all things,
> > > wherever you may place me
> > > in all that I do and in all that I may endure;
> > > when there is work for me and when there is none;
> > > when I am troubled and when I am at peace;
> > Your will be done
> > > when I am valued and when I am disregarded;
> > > when I find fulfilment and when it is lacking;
> > > when I have all things and when I have nothing.
> > I willingly offer all I have and am
> > > to serve you, as and where you choose.

Glorious and blessed God, Father, Son and Holy Spirit,
you are mine and I am yours.
May it be so for ever.
Let this covenant now made on earth be fulfilled in heaven.
Amen.[18]

The journey towards holiness is one that must involve our whole selves. The holy is not a separate part of the world; it permeates the whole of our universe, and so it must transform the whole of our lives.

The journey towards holiness is one in which we must empty ourselves of our own ambitions and aims, however good we may think them, because holiness is always beyond anything we can aim at. To paraphrase T. S. Eliot's paraphrase of John of the Cross: 'if you want to arrive at what you are not, you have to go through the way in which you are not'.[19]

It is only as we are able to place ourselves freely into God's hands, which is a slow and hard process, that we can be filled with God.

But that is our aim: to allow ourselves to be more and more filled with God, so that the people we serve may be able to detect in us at least the memory of the aroma of God. Then as we celebrate the eucharist with them, and as we preach, and as we serve, we are bringing them not into our own presence but into the presence of the living God.

Priest and community

As those of you who can still remember the first chapter will know, when I was an ordinand preparing for ministry, I went on placement to a large and successful Catholic parish. Not being a naturally tactful person, I answered truthfully when the vicar asked me for my reflections on the Church Council meeting I sat in on. As far as I could see, the only really important item on the agenda was called 'Vicar's notices', which was the point at which he told everyone else what was going to happen. As I got to know the parish, I realized quite a lot of the lay people in the church quite liked it that way, because it meant they never had to take responsibility for anything, and if it went wrong they wouldn't be to blame.

That's one version of the Catholic priest, colloquially known as 'Father knows best'. It won't do. Leadership in a postmodern world is about giving meaning, not orders. The task of a leader in church is first to hold the boundaries of the body, to give it a meaningful shape. This means having a clear idea of what this body looks like, and what it might look like in the future. It's not just a question of having a great vision of the church as you would like it to be; it also requires realism about the church as it is now. And even in the process of developing and articulating a vision, the whole church needs to be joining in the task – even though that will undoubtedly mean that bits of the vision will not be what the leader would like. Leadership is as much about negotiating the possible into the visionary as anything else. And leadership is about taking the risk of sharing leadership, and enabling others to take leadership roles with real responsibility.

That doesn't mean that the priest becomes no more than a facilitator; there is a distinctively theological role that the Christian community needs as it discerns its vocation. Bauman again poses the problem: 'the ethical paradox of the postmodern condition is that it restores to agents the fullness of moral choice and responsibility while simultaneously depriving them of the comfort of the universal guidance that modern self-confidence once promised. Ethical tasks of individuals grow while the socially produced resources to fulfil them shrink.'[20] Priests are called to help individuals into the community of faith, and to help that community discern within the tradition what its calling is in the present moment.

The Church needs to find itself again as a body in which power is continually on the move – when it stays in one place, it quickly goes stale. For one final example of possible ways of working, it may be worth turning to some of the new ways that businesses have developed in responding to the changes in their commercial environment. In a few places, desks have gone, individual work stations are a thing of the past, and work can be done as much around the pool table as the data projector. But those are just the cosmetic aspects: the real revolution is in the management structure which those changes (hopefully) represent. Rather than a management setting objectives and apportioning tasks, the role of leadership in this sort of institution is to create climate, to maintain atmosphere, and to engender trust. Not words normally associated with senior managers in secular or sacred institutions. But it is a model that enables the loosing of power. Individuals are not restricted by a job description that requires them to do certain things and prevents them from doing many others. They can join a group working on a certain project, and bring their distinctive gifts to bear on it, and then move on to something else. Others will naturally be more inclined to stick with one project and see it through from start to finish. 'We have gifts that differ'[21] – let's not spend most of our time using gifts we haven't got.

The loosing of power can only take place within an organization whose structures are organic and flexible: not fluid, still firmly connected, but the whole able to change in response to change in any part of the organism. The conditions for that sort of organism are open communication, genuine trust and, most importantly, a clear sense of common purpose. It is those that leaders can foster, or destroy, usually thinking that they are fulfilling their prime responsibility. 'When leaders strive for equilibrium and stability by imposing control, constricting people's freedom and inhibiting local change, they only create the conditions that threaten the organisation's survival.'[22]

There's no need for church leaders to worry about the fact that their co-workers in the church are all volunteers, unless they think they are unlikely to be able to inspire them or enable them to feel involved. It is always those who regard their work as something that they want to do for its own and their own sake who get the job done, whether they are being paid for it or not. 'Power is the capacity generated by our relationships'[23] – in the end it resides in our ability to get other people to do things. And, paradoxically, the best way to get people to do things is to inspire them with a vision, give them the tools and set them free. Jesus did not run training sessions for the disciples on what they should do or not do, the finer points of evangelism and the principles of church growth. He (literally) inspired them, and told them to go out. And they went.

5

God's joyful work: Worship

The Parish Masses (and more)

It has been one of the assumptions of the churches in the last couple of generations that the perfect form of the Christian assembly was when the maximum number of people were gathered together to worship, following the same liturgy in the same place at the same time. Clergy have been heard to claim proudly that they have managed to close down all their services except the Sunday morning Parish Mass. One of the results has been that many people, in the cities especially, assume that all the churches in their locality are closed: Christians, footballers and exceptionally keen shoppers are nowadays almost the only people up and about on a Sunday morning. More importantly, as society has changed, a single form and time and space for worship has become less and less likely to attract the diversity of groups of which society is now composed. Diversity is now one of the key terms for understanding contemporary life: the local church, meanwhile, is still trying to persuade its worshippers to conform to a single pattern of worship.

This is classic modernism: that which postmodernity particularly revolts against. The idea that there is one (identifiable) locus of truth, to which all things refer, is a classic case of logocentrism. It's shown in the 'proper' way of doing church architecture as well – out must go the side chapels, the extra decorations, the distractions of 'Catholic tat', to be replaced by clear and easily understood structures, pointing unambiguously to the key liturgical places, the place of the reading of the Scriptures, the font and the altar especially. Given that traditional Catholic styles of worship had, quite openly, rejected the whole movement called modernism, it is ironic that the gift that modernism brought was only embraced just as postmodernism was beginning to stir. It is difficult to disagree with the Second Vatican Council's pronouncement:

> In order that the Christian people may more certainly derive an abundance of graces from the sacred liturgy, holy Mother Church desires to undertake with great care a general restoration of the liturgy itself. For the liturgy is made up of immutable elements divinely instituted, and of elements subject to change. These not only may but ought to be changed with the passage of time if they have suffered from the intrusion of anything out of harmony with the inner nature of the liturgy or have become unsuited to it.
>
> In this restoration, both texts and rites should be drawn up so that they express more clearly the holy things which they signify; the Christian people, so far as possible, should be enabled to understand them with ease and to take part in them fully, actively, and as befits a community.[1]

The Tridentine Mass[2] certainly needed development, but the form the development took was to embrace a world-view that was just beginning to pass away – the Second Vatican Council commenced in 1962, the same year as a young philosopher called Jacques Derrida began to appear in print.

In the Church of England, this modernist revolution in the Roman Catholic Church was one of the causes of the fragmentation of the Catholic tradition. On the one hand were those who accepted the authority of Rome completely – so if Rome dictated a complete change in the liturgy, so be it. On the other hand, there were those (like the similar rebels within Roman Catholicism) who were convinced that the Tridentine Mass, and the liturgical style and practices that went with it, were not merely an expression of worship, but the heart of it: the whole package was as one, and it shouldn't be changed.

To add to the confusion, by this time in the Church of England the Parish Communion was making great headway. Regarded as a cop-out by 'proper' Anglo-Catholics, it introduced to the wider Church of England a way in which Communion could become the normal Sunday service. The classic Anglo-Catholic practice had been to come twice: to receive communion (fasting, of course) at the 8 o'clock Low Mass, and to attend, but not receive, at the 11 o'clock Solemn Mass. 'The Lord's people at the Lord's table on the Lord's day' was a way into a modified Catholicism, with a service at around 9 o'clock, followed in the early days by a parish breakfast. As the movement spread beyond those who took fasting communion seriously, of course the hour could move later and the incentive for the breakfast disappeared.

The classic text for all this was *The Parish Communion*.[3] For me it is ironic that its editor, A. G. Hebert, points out that a Church divided theologically and geographically is still united in Christ, but nevertheless presses the case for a single parish eucharist (if at all possible) in each parish.[4]

More pragmatically, the Parish Communion movement was a way of theologizing the decline in attendance which had begun to be noticeable,[5] and an opportunity to rationalize the various children's services, choral matins and so on which had become perceived as an encumbrance to ministry. The parish priest's role was to get all his people to gather together for the communion in order to create a sense of the worshipping community as a distinct body.

The Parish Eucharist has become the norm for many Anglicans who wouldn't at all wear the label 'Catholic'. One service each Sunday, with a liturgy in clear and contemporary language, in an environment stripped of extraneous clutter: it has also become the norm for those Catholics who regard themselves as being in touch with the contemporary world. If only. Just as the Church has simplified, the world around us has got interested again in the messy, the temporary, the complex. That doesn't mean a return to pre-modern styles of worship – except for the occasional visit, which is a completely different thing. The pre-modern Tridentine style was hugely rich and also completely fixed: one had to buy the whole package or nothing. Postmodernity loves flexibility, contingency, a responsiveness to local conditions and the immediate situation. Of course that can lead to simplicity – the eucharist described in chapter 2 is simple in the extreme – but the next night might have something completely different. There is always the possibility of another perspective, of another meaning.

But is it right?

It's all very well to say that modernist styles of worship (or pre-modern ones, for that matter) don't work in the postmodern world. That doesn't answer the question, especially for Catholics. Ways of worship aren't purely pragmatic, any more than modes of structuring the Church are. Worship is *opus dei* – the work of God (no, this isn't a reference to the organization of the same name). That means that we don't worship in order to gain a personal positive experience, and services of worship are not designed solely to attract as many people as possible. Worship is the offering of the creature to the creator, and its first focus must be on God, not on ourselves.[6]

Trying to clear away the habits of centuries, and the theological justifications for them, is hard work, and would take far too long to be attempted in this book. I'll just have to leave all the liturgists out there really angry and frustrated, and cut to the key point as I see it. There isn't one form of liturgy that is specifically ordained by God – what there are are the sacraments, key places where we know we will meet God. Those promises remain constant, and should be the magnetic poles that we cannot resist as Christian people, the places where we are drawn again and again. But how they might be manifested is infinitely various. It's not liturgies that matter (well, they do, but not quite as much), but the sacramental life of the community which they embody and express.

This is the place where my experience of alternative worship, and a traditional Catholic view of worship, seem to come into most direct conflict. From alternative worship, I got the principles that traditional texts and actions are resources, not rules, and that visual images, and the other senses, are much more prominent. Also in chapter 2, though, Charles Gore seemed to be describing a system in which there is a clear and unambiguous channel running between the heavenly and earthly realms, through which divine grace can be guaranteed to flow – and demanding that all Christian people must engage in this way with these activities, or they're not part of the community any more.

But I think there is a way through here, by developing further the question I asked in chapter 2: 'How many *sacraments* are there anyway?' It may strike those of you not familiar with the history as a really odd question, a very strange place to start when dealing with the way we meet God. I think you're right – and the fact that this is an issue just demonstrates the ways in which the need for order and control has dominated discussion, and narrowed our understanding of God's generosity. The Orthodox Churches have generally been much less obsessive about this sort of thing. Here's a very different way of approaching the whole matter:

> [T]he world is symbolical . . . in virtue of its being created by God . . . It is then the 'natural' symbolism of the world – one can almost say its 'sacramentality' – that makes the sacrament *possible* and constitutes the key to its understanding and apprehension. If the Christian sacrament is unique, it is not in the sense of being a miraculous exception to the natural order of things created by God and 'proclaiming his glory'. The 'mysterion' [mystery, the Orthodox word for sacrament] of Christ reveals and fulfills the ultimate meaning and destiny of the world itself.[7]

That expresses for me a key truth that translates from the pre-modernism of Orthodox doctrine into a postmodern Catholicity, without getting caught up in modernist arguments on the way. Re-understanding sacraments from a postmodern perspective can help us to move away from numbering the ways in which God is at work. Sacrament can become a way of thinking about how God is at work in the world, how the presence of God is diffused and dispersed into the world God loves. Far from being points of control, the withholding of which excludes people from God's presence, the sacraments as such are pointers towards the sacramentality of all things: specific places through which the presence of God which is everywhere is felt in a specific time and event.

Maybe it's worthwhile remembering one of the great purple passages of liturgical theology, now I suspect slipping into forgetfulness, the final paragraph of Gregory Dix's *The Shape of the Liturgy*:

[Jesus] had told his friends to do this henceforward with the new meaning 'for the anamnesis' of Him, and they have done it always since.

Was ever another command so obeyed? For century after century, spreading slowly to every continent and country and among every race on earth, this action has been done, in every conceivable human circumstance, for every conceivable human need from infancy and before it to extreme old age and after it, from the pinnacles of earthly greatness to the refuges of fugitives in caves and the dens of the earth. Men have found no better thing than this to do for kings at their crowning and for criminals going to the scaffold; for armies in triumph or for a bride and bridegroom in a little country church; for the proclamation of a dogma or for a good crop of wheat; for the wisdom of the Parliament of a mighty nation or for a sick old woman afraid to die; for a schoolboy sitting an examination or for Columbus setting out to discover America; for the famine of whole provinces or for the soul of a dead lover; in thankfulness because my father did not die of pneumonia; for a village headman much tempted to return to fetish because the yams have failed; because the Turk was at the gates of Vienna; for the repentance of Margaret; for the settlement of a strike; for a son for a barren woman; for Captain so-and-so, wounded and prisoner of war; while the lions roared in the nearby amphitheatre; on the beach at Dunkirk; while the hiss of scythes in the thick June grass came faintly through the windows of the church; tremulously, by an old monk on the fiftieth anniversary of his vows; furtively, by an exiled bishop who had hewn timber all day in a prison camp near Murmansk; gorgeously, for the canonisation of S. Joan of Arc – one could fill many pages with the reasons why men have done this, and not tell a hundredth part of them. And best of all, week by week and month by month, on a hundred thousand successive Sundays, faithfully, unfailingly, across all the parishes of Christendom, the pastors have done this just to make the *plebs sancta Dei* – the holy common people of God.[8]

I don't suppose Dix would be very happy at my taking it that way, but for me that passage speaks most powerfully about how varied and contextual is the sacramental life of the people of God – and that the primary sacraments are so important as pointers towards the greater mystery of the incarnation, that God has worked his greatest work in his Son, fully human as well as fully God.

The sort of approach to liturgy that I'm suggesting seems to me to fit hand in glove with a vision of the incarnation in which the body of Christ is dissolved kenotically into the world,[9] so that it is continually entering into dialogue with the other stories that compete to make sense of the world around us. The sacraments are at the heart of that story, being re-told in ever new ways. But that re-telling, if it is to be true to its context, cannot be too constrained by restriction on text or on context. We have to take the risk of setting the sacramental life free, modelled on the risk God took in letting his own life be shared with the life of his creation. Anything the Church does as

Church is somehow sacramental: that is a challenge and a vision for postmodern worship.

It may involve a rather unusual interpretation, but I don't believe anything I'm saying here contradicts the fundamental (Roman) Catholic doctrines of the sacraments.[10] The sacraments undoubtedly flow from Christ – not in the sense of needing to find (or make up) an instance when he directly told his followers to do a certain thing in a certain way, but because he is the first and greatest sacrament. He confers the grace he signifies – which is the second characteristic of a sacrament. It's important to remain supernaturalist about sacraments; if they are merely signs of human activity they are no longer integrally linked to Christ *as events*. My only difference is over that question of number: sure, there are seven sacraments; just don't stop there, keep on counting.

Another key aspect of Catholic teaching is that three sacraments 'confer a character' – they change the person who has received them: baptism, confirmation and ordination. Therefore they are not repeatable: once done, they are done. That idea of permanence challenges the postmodern cult of personal authenticity. How can baptism mean anything to a child too young to know what's going on? The very question presupposes the individual as the author of the truth of his or her own life. But it is the very challenge of sacramentality that is the offering the Church has to give a society fixated with individualistic authenticity as its sole criterion. It's God who acts, whatever the intention or the holiness of the minister of the sacrament. Otherwise we're allowing the tests of personal authenticity into the equation. The sacraments are God's action, not ours.

Patterns of worship

Writing in around AD 156, Justin Martyr wrote: 'when we have finished praying, bread and wine and water are brought up, and the president likewise sends up prayers and thanksgivings to the best of his ability, and the people assent, saying the Amen'.[11] That's one of the earliest descriptions of a Christian eucharist, and that's the pattern I think should be our inspiration in understanding the future of sacramental worship. It's not the ideal that churches have worked with up to now; in fact, the key person has been someone else, Hippolytus, who gave a much more detailed description, including pretty much the full text of a eucharistic prayer. Hippolytus has been incredibly important in the modernist phase of the Church's life, when everything's been simplified and focused. His prayer has been used as a basis for new prayers which have been used by many churches.

It was all very well for modern times; in postmodernism we have to have a lot more flexibility. Justin Martyr's description makes it clear that the priest wasn't just reading from a set text; he (and it was a 'he' of course) was expected to find his own words to express the community's praise and the promise of God's presence. That sort of thing causes a lot of anxiety among the churches. In fact, there was a very tentative proposal in the Church of England to have an order for the eucharist that consisted more of instructions (rubrics as we like to call them in the Church) than texts.[12] It never even saw the light of day. There's a lot of fear involved in setting free the sacraments from specific texts, but that's exactly what we need to do – and we need priests and communities capable of doing the job.

One of the phrases that has been somewhat disparaged in relation to liturgical diversity is 'family resemblance'. But that's what we need – coherence, not identity. If we are to remain one body of Christ, our worship must exhibit family resemblance, but not be a series of clones. Sadly it doesn't seem to be the way the wind is blowing at present. One of the Vatican's recent pronouncements on liturgy[13] seemed to be deliberately intended to roll back from the small stirrings of a response to postmodern times. It is as if the Tradition had to be protected from those whose task it is to make it come alive in the present day – the worshipping communities of the Church.

Liturgy which grows out of the experience of the local community, and which is moreover creative and innovative, is exactly what the alternative worship tradition is known for, so it's not surprising that I'm going to suggest the rest of us have a lot to learn here. Some of what its proponents have to say is not all that flattering:

> In some cases old rituals have been allowed to dry up and lose their meaning. Our experience has been that taking them on and reinventing them, playing with them, making connections with contemporary life, reinvesting them with meaning is very exciting. They come alive in unprecedented ways . . . the intense interest of alt.worship groups in ritual does not often extend to the tight liturgical codes of many high church practitioners.[14]

Well, that's told us – but we need to be told. When confronted by something new, what do we high church practitioners do? Complain that rituals aren't being used as the rule book says they should? We need to get real – the rule book is a myth anyway.

One of the bits of my history I haven't mentioned before illustrated this for me. For a few years I was occupied teaching men and women preparing for ordained ministry. Every year we would celebrate a High Mass, so that everyone on the course got a little taste of what it was like, and those who were from a Catholic tradition (all of them Anglicans) had a brief moment of enjoying worship done in the way they were used to at home. We would gather the students together, and talk through what we were going to do. Most of them were servers or otherwise involved in the worship of their home churches, so they all had a pretty good idea of 'how it should be done'. Some of them even had notes from their incumbents specially for the occasion. Needless to say, all the versions were different and often mutually incompatible. The only time when liturgical and ritualistic worship is done well is not when it follows the rubrics of a book but when it brings the tradition intelligently to bear on the needs of the community.

There's a well-established model of professional work that suits well what we need in church communities, and especially among those who lead liturgy – that of the reflective practitioner. The main name in this field is Donald Schon.[15] Schon suggests:

> The practitioner allows himself to experience surprise, puzzlement, or confusion in a situation which he finds uncertain or unique. He reflects on the phenomenon before him, and on the prior understandings which have been implicit in his behaviour. He carries out an experiment which serves to generate both a new understanding of the phenomenon and a change in the situation.[16]

> When a practitioner makes sense of a situation he perceives to be unique, he *sees* it *as* something already present in his repertoire. To see *this* site as *that* one is not to subsume the first under a familiar category or rule. It is, rather, to see the unfamiliar, unique situation as both similar to and different from the familiar one, without at first being able to say similar or different with respect to what. The familiar situation functions as a precedent, or a metaphor, or . . . an exemplar for the unfamiliar one.[17]

I wouldn't exactly describe the Christian tradition as a repertoire, but it's close enough to work with. Schon's description fits exactly with what the Church needs to be as it develops its worshipping and sacramental life. We need clergy who are able to improvise – using and in coherence with the tradition – and able to do the interpretive work of applying the tradition to their situation. Priests need to be skilled performers, 'stand-up theologians', responding to their congregation as a good stand-up comic responds to an audience – and with the additional gift of the Holy Spirit's grace enabling them to do so.

Developing this sort of skill base among the communities of faith – and particularly among those who preside over worship – is a major task. Having (as you know) for a brief while attended a charismatic house church I can testify from personal experience that many people are not very good at discerning the 'feel' – the Spirit's movement even – in an act of worship. It can be done, and it can be taught, but the implications for training clergy and lay ministers, and for the writing of liturgy, would be immense. We would need to move unashamedly away from a 'university degree' model of theological education, and embrace what some have begun to explore, a fully practical approach. It wouldn't be a dumbing down, though, as anyone can see who can understand the complexity of enabling liturgy through improvisation rather than obedience to texts. The risks are real, but the rewards are greater – the reward of a liturgy able to be transformed into being the people's offering of praise in each place, while also taking its place coherently within the worship of the whole Church Catholic.

Just one example, very simple, from St Mary's, Stoke Newington of how we played with the liturgy. In the autumn of 2007, we decided to dedicate one of our weekday evening eucharists to the Millennium Development Goals, and our collective commitment to seeing them come about. So we used readings from a variety of sources as well as Scripture, and when it came to the part of the service normally occupied by the intercessions, those present were invited to pray at a number of stations around the church, each focused on one goal. The one on child mortality was an empty double buggy, emblazoned with the statistics; the one on HIV/AIDS featured condoms as well as meditations. So far, so moderately adventurous. But for the Eucharistic Prayer, we were invited to gather around one of the stations, the one dedicated to relief of hunger. It was an ordinary folding table, with several places set, only one of which had any food on it. And when it came to the communion, the priest gave communion only to a quarter of those present. I knew it was going to happen, but even so it blew my mind, to kneel there and not receive the sacrament while others did. The starkness of injustice was never so personal for me. Then, after a pause for reflection, we all stood and affirmed our commitment to justice for all people – and the rest of us received communion.

I could go on and on, but there are loads of places to look, in print or on the internet, for examples of liturgy testing the boundaries.[18] Anyway, what I'm trying to do here is not to provide answers – that would be rather contrary to my whole argument – but to stimulate thought, and prayer, about how worship might develop where you are.

Confession and all that

As you may remember, I trained for ordination at an evangelical theological college. On Mondays at 5 p. m. we had an act of worship which was called Exposition. The first time I mentioned it to the Anglo-Catholic vicar of the church where I worshipped, he was considerably surprised – until he realized that it was a scriptural exposition, a good hour's biblical teaching. Exposition of the Blessed Sacrament, on the other hand, is a rather different matter. With varying degrees of splendour and good taste, the sacramental wafer is removed from the tabernacle in which is it kept, and shown to the people for adoration and devotion. There's plenty more: a huge variety of spiritual practices which have grown up, especially around the Sacrament and the Blessed Virgin Mary, and also around the saints, their places of birth and martyrdom, their relics and places of miracle.

In a postmodern age, the last thing we need to feel is embarrassed about all this. It's a rich seam of resource for re-making. These liturgies which surround the core sacraments of the Church grew up incrementally in response to the needs at the time of the worshipping community. They wouldn't go down very well in modernism, because they don't make sense in a closed system of cause and effect, they have no purchase at all on a rationalist mindset. But they are great for creating atmosphere, for liberating emotion. Benediction is the only space in which I've seen Anglo-Catholic clergy worshipping with almost the fervour of charismatics, suddenly revealing a talent for extemporary prayer that was otherwise kept well under wraps.

As well as the more public and flamboyant side of Catholic worship, there's another key gift – a core sacrament – which is increasingly rarely practised: the sacrament of reconciliation, which most people still think of as 'confession'. Despite my disagreements elsewhere, I think Pete Ward comes up with a brilliant way of re-connecting the sacrament with contemporary life, even if he doesn't appear to be completely aware of the fact. He talks about the culture of personal fitness, of individualized trainers, and suggests that the Church should offer spirituality fitness check-ups.[19] Shorn of its associations with humiliation and punishment, that's exactly what reconciliation offers. Individuals have time to reflect on the deepest spiritual realities of their lives, to receive healing through absolution and to hear a prescription for spiritual wellness. We might need a new liturgy, though, and a way of setting the sacrament that was neither the hierarchical model of the confessional, nor the doctor's consulting room model favoured in contemporary Roman Catholic churches, almost devoid of spirituality. Perhaps the Orthodox practice might work, in which priest and penitent stand together before an icon: in the solidarity of their humanity.

Holy spaces

This section could be a book in itself, so I'll try to keep it as brief as I can. Church buildings and spaces for worship – how do our medieval, or Victorian, or modern spaces respond to a postmodern culture? If Christian space is primarily about people, its buildings are theatres, not monuments: they are spaces for possibility, places of exploration. They exist for what they make possible, not what they do in themselves. Therefore any church that gives the illusion of being complete merely as a building is heretical – it's saying that God has been understood, and everything is sorted.

Well, that's a bit extreme, but that's the danger of an authoritarian architecture: a building that dictates what you can or can't do by its very shape. On the other hand, and this is why we need architects, an empty room scarcely conveys anything of the Tradition of the faith. It's a lot easier to build a church when 'everyone' knows what sort of thing you should do in it, and what you shouldn't.

The Victorian Anglo-Catholic movement was closely entwined with the re-discovery of Gothic church architecture: the only proper form for a building of worship, as they thought. The long chancel leads up to a sanctuary raised up above the congregation in the nave, creating a space of holy mystery within which the sacred moments can be seen but only at a distance, as the priest raises the sacrament above his head, amid clouds of incense, at the high altar. Statues and side chapels proliferated as secondary foci to that one act which defined the space as holy.

Not so in liturgical modernism. When you've got the font, the lectern, the altar all in the right place and relationship, you've made the space for worship. The altar is placed so that the priest stands behind it and the people aren't too far away. It's still the primary focus, but the places of baptism and the proclamation of the word are also given due prominence in the main body of the church. Everything else should be as plain as possible so that the eye and the spiritual attentiveness are focused on only those key elements.

It may be a lot emptier than a Gothic space, but liturgical modernism isn't truly flexible. It doesn't allow for the time when you want for once to use a completely different shape, or want to fill the space with light – or darkness, or helium-filled bàlloons for that matter. There is nothing more dictatorial than a truly minimal modernist space. In postmodern times we need spaces that are responsive, multi-faceted. Regardless of what the leaders of worship might want to do, the people of God should be trusted – God should be trusted – to make their own connections. The meaning of an act of worship can't in fact be controlled, however much we simplify, it can only be denuded. In creating spaces within which worship can happen, we have to leave it up to the Spirit – making spaces in which God can be at work. In a eucharist, that means that the Tradition gives us a shape, a purpose, and a huge resource of texts – but there needs to be more freedom in how those key points of encounter with word and sacrament are expressed in any given service. The Church of England has managed to give this sort of freedom to non-eucharistic services: in order for the Catholic tradition to be able to respond to the times in which we live, the same freedom needs to be given to eucharistic worship.

Having in many cases got rid of all the liturgical clutter, we need again to have images, side altars, chapels for this or that – all creating possibilities for people to find their own niche, their own space for worship. Again, the pre-modern and the postmodern connect up; in an Orthodox service, the congregation are able to wander from icon to icon, to make their own prayers in tune with the liturgy, but not necessarily identically to the liturgy. The difference is that in postmodernity the scenery can all be shifted.

Keeping it all together

The danger of all this is that the church's life becomes so diffuse and diverse that religion is just a pick-and-mix spiritual experience. How do we keep it all together? Here the role of priests and other leaders is really key; they need to be 'scribes who bring out things both old and new' from the treasury of the Tradition,[20] and maintain the boundaries of faith – not through trying to enforce doctrinal assent, nor through preventing independence of thought and feeling, but through a common structure of sacramental participation.

It is in sharing together in the same sacramental body – by doing the same things, even if clothed in a variety of expressions – that we remain one body of Christ. A postmodern body, which doesn't necessarily have to wear matching clothes, in which mutual recognition is achieved not through assent to external criteria, but through a network of relationships constantly renewed. A body which doesn't even need (*pace* the Parish Communion movement) to meet together in the same service at the same time every week, as long as its unity is held by the common relationship to priest and to bishop. Finally – and leading neatly into the next chapter – a body of people who find their common faith lived out in their common service to the world.

6

Left a bit, left a bit:
the Church political

Seek ye first the divine society and the divine justice, and all these things – clothes more beautiful than Solomon's, and good food and drink – shall be added unto you. Be social, godly, just, and you shall have Utopia.[1]

Men may celebrate no second centenary of our movement if we do not determine now to stand in social and doctrinal issues plainly upon our own ground, with a message and a philosophy for the whole range of human life, and a true order of ends and values, which men may reject indeed, but the distinctive character of which they can no longer mistake.[2]

The second quotation above is doubly quoted; the speaker was Maurice Reckitt, an Anglo-Catholic Socialist of the first half of the twentieth century, who spoke these words in 1933, the centenary year of the Oxford Movement. He was quoted by Kenneth Leech and Rowan Williams in their introduction to *Essays Catholic and Radical*, published in 1983, the 150th anniversary year. It is symptomatic of the problems in the Catholic tradition that I want to talk about in this chapter that this was not the 'official' commemoration. The official events also produced a book, the prevailing tone of which, despite its title, is a reflective and scholarly affection for something that is no longer what it was.[3] Trevor Huddleston's sermon at the service of commemoration did attempt to push the Catholic tradition beyond its own internal concerns, by exploring the true meaning of the word 'Catholic': 'If we are *truly* Catholic, the universality – the proclamation of our belief that this is God's world, God's universe – is surely a prior concern to that which would make institutional Christianity our chief objective.'[4] Unfortunately it would seem his sermon had as little effect on the wider movement as Leech and Williams' book.

One of the chapters of *Essays Catholic and Radical* is entitled 'Behold I am doing a new thing'[5] – a title which sums up the difference in intent between the two anniversary publications. Both express a sense of crisis within the Catholic tradition in the Church of England; only *Essays Catholic and Radical* appears to have some vision for the future. It's a generalization, of course, and there are counter-examples in each book. But overall I think it holds, and it indicates something profound about the weaknesses of the Catholic tradition, that it was finally being overwhelmed, as Rowan Williams and Ken Leech wrote, by a 'steady retreat towards preoccupations of a mainly ecclesiastical nature . . . it is hard to avoid the impression of a degree of isolation from the wider world in a lot of Catholic activity'.[6]

By the 1980s, Anglo-Catholics were reaping the fruit of the prophetic words spoken by Bishop Frank Weston at the 1923 Anglo-Catholic Congress, words famous but not much obeyed, of which I have already quoted a few. Here is a longer excerpt:

> You cannot claim to worship Jesus in the Tabernacle, if you do not pity Jesus in the slum . . . Now mark that – this is the Gospel truth. If you are prepared to say that the Anglo-Catholic is at perfect liberty to rake in all the money he can get no matter what the wages are that are paid, no matter what the conditions are under which people work; if you say that the Anglo-Catholic has a right to hold his peace while his fellow citizens are living in hovels below the levels of the streets, this I say to you, that you do not yet know the Lord Jesus in his Sacrament. You have begun with the Christ of Bethlehem, you have gone on to know something of the Christ of Calvary – but

the Christ of the Sacrament, not yet. Oh brethren! if only you listen tonight your movement is going to sweep England. If you listen. I am not talking economics, I do not understand them. I am not talking politics, I do not understand them. I am talking the Gospel, and I say to you this: If you are Christians then your Jesus is one and the same: Jesus on the Throne of his glory, Jesus in the Blessed Sacrament, Jesus received into your hearts in Communion, Jesus with you mystically as you pray, and Jesus enthroned in the hearts and bodies of his brothers and sisters up and down this country. And it is folly – it is madness – to suppose that you can worship Jesus in the Sacraments and Jesus on the Throne of glory, when you are sweating him in the souls and bodies of his children. It cannot be done . . . Go out and look for Jesus in the ragged, in the naked, in the oppressed and sweated, in those who have lost hope, in those who are struggling to make good. Look for Jesus. And when you see him, gird yourselves with his towel and try to wash their feet.[7]

The failure to live out a Catholic theology that had a theologically formed vision of how to engage with the needs of a changing society eventually left Anglo-Catholics marooned on the dissolving sandbank of the institution of the Church, which was and is increasingly uninteresting to most people.

It'll be apparent by now that the only sort of political involvement I can conceive of as representing a Christian commitment is at least somewhere to the left of the political middle. The parish of which I am presently the parish priest has a rather splendid banner; its last two outings from church were on the Stop the War march against the UK's involvement in the Second Iraq War, and the march commemorating the bicentenary of the abolition of the slave trade. In fairness, I should say that I know there are equally devout Christians (some in my parish) who see Conservatism as the only possible vehicle for expressing their faith in the public realm. I acknowledge it to be so, but without any idea of how the connection is made. So here I shall speak out of my own convictions.

Where did it all go wrong?

We looked at some of the roots of all this in the first chapter. Just to recap on where we'd got to at that point: on the one hand there was the defining characteristic of Anglo-Catholicism identified by K. E. Kirk at the 33rd Anglo-Catholic Congress: *the social mission of the Church*. He describes a mission based on the doctrine of the incarnation, which showed 'that there is no sphere of human affairs, however mundane, civic, or commercial, which is without the possibility of being sanctified by the Holy Spirit, as the human nature of Christ was sanctified by the indwelling word of God'.[8] It was a mission worked out in practice, in the sacrificial service of priests, religious brothers and sisters, and lay people in the worst slums. It was a mission that was without illusions about human sinfulness: Anglo-Catholics knew that 'the sacramental grace of God' was as necessary as the relief of material poverty.

If all of that was as key to Anglo-Catholic life as Kirk suggests, it requires a word or two of explanation as to why it became increasingly marginal to the movement as a whole. For that we can return again to chapter 1, and Kenneth Leech's analysis of the movement's weakness, which had a particular impact on mission. First, never pulling any punches, there's Leech's contention that the 'organic and rigidly hierarchical view of both church and society . . . veers towards a kind of fascism . . . Many Anglo-Catholics, particularly those of a Papalist outlook, have shared in this view of the social order.' When that is added to the Anglo-Catholic tendency to create 'a world within a world', less and less related to the world of reality, the ingredients are all in place for a comfort zone of churchy life which can block out the changing society of which it is part.[9] We noted the consequences of this for the Church's own internal life in the previous chapter, but it's equally fatal for the Church's attempts to look out beyond its own borders.

As we noted also in chapter 1, there was a succession of groupings that saw a socialist vision of society as an essential part of Catholic faith. 'Christianity is the religion of which socialism is the practice'[10] expressed the conviction of those on the inside, but they remained, through all the various manifestations of the movement, a small minority, never managing to convince the majority of Anglo-Catholics, let alone those in the wider Church.

In *Essays Catholic and Radical*, John Orens charts the efforts and the failures of the Anglo-Catholic Socialists up to the 1923 Congress. In doing so, he also uncovers some of the fundamental theological principles that will need to underpin any renewed Catholic commitment to social action. His principal hero is Stewart Headlam, the turbulent priest whom he sees as 'the father of the modern Christian Socialist movement'.[11] Headlam brought together two strands: the thought of F. D. Maurice, in 'his explanation of baptismal regeneration, his belief that the Incarnation hallows every human faculty and concern, and his insistence that the Kingdom of God is to come on earth'.[12] But Headlam saw all these things as making sense only in the context of a Catholic doctrinal and liturgical framework, and linked essentially to the life of faith. He was no theological liberal, even in nineteenth-century terms. By uniting Maurice's incarnational emphasis with an uncompromisingly Catholic approach, he argued that he was proposing a renewed vision for Catholics, one that would be much more likely to be effective than the exceedingly sober spirituality of the first Tractarians. 'We exist not only to bring about the economic revolution but to maintain and where necessary to revive the great institution of the Church . . . for the Church alone is the divine society founded to struggle against evil and usher in the Kingdom of God.'[13]

For Headlam and others it was obvious that the path to the Kingdom of heaven lay through socialism. One, writing (supposedly) of the Early Fathers, said: 'When the writer is sound and saintly, then he is always entirely and unhesitatingly in favour of common holding of goods, of equality of opportunity, of social freedom . . .'.[14] In the early twenty-first century, that equation is perhaps rather less obvious. There was a good deal of modernism as well as of theology in the programme of the early Anglo-Catholic Socialists. Their (various) programmes set out an authoritarian vision of the good society, itself firmly rooted in the unquestioned authority of the Church. It is symptomatic that one of the volumes of essays that sought to recall the church to socialism was entitled *The Return of Christendom*.[15]

Donald Gray argues strongly for a connection between the 'sacramental socialists' and the development of the Parish Communion movement, which I mentioned in a previous chapter, on the grounds that it represents a real connection with the sacramental life of the Church: '[T]hey saw the People of God around the Altar on a Sunday morning as preparing themselves for whatever political or social action they were to be called to in the coming week.'[16]

Although some of those involved in the early Parish Communion movement were undoubtedly socialists, the movement did not in fact energize the Church widely for social engagement. It might be truer to say that it was part of a withdrawal of the Church from the public realm as churchgoing ceased to be the social norm, and the church had to re-imagine itself as a gathered community rather than reflecting the whole population of its parish (or at least those who hadn't opted in to another form of church).

The latest incarnation of Anglo-Catholic Socialism is the Society of Sacramental Socialists. Their website sets out the basis of my own commitment too:

> We believe that God is by nature fundamentally engaged with the world and on the side of poor and oppressed people.
> This understanding is rooted in the:

- words of Holy Scripture,
- Holy Mass, which establishes the equality of all people,
- writings of the Mothers and Fathers of the Faith,
- tradition of the Communion of the Saints,
- historic doctrines of the Holy Church,
- relationship of perfect and equal love displayed in the Holy Trinity,
- vulnerable love exemplified in the person of Jesus Christ.[17]

It is profoundly un-Catholic for the Church to be concerned only for itself. Those who are called into Christ's family are not called into a closed shop of the elect, but into a company of disciples whose calling is to serve the world around them. Catholics should, if we were to live out our own vocation, have a vision of mission which did not exclude, but included and surpassed, the conversion of individuals, and went on to work for the transformation of the world. We are now being put to shame by those we have criticized for their individualism, because many evangelicals are now more Catholic than we are in their practical commitment to social action.

There is at one level a very natural connection between Anglo-Catholicism and traditional socialism. Both are ideologies that are completely sure about the right of certain people (whether the Church, or the working classes) to hold and use power in society. Whether it's 'all power to the masses' or 'all power in the Mass', there is no theoretical issue involved. Lots of practical difficulties in making it happen, but that's different. Once the holding of power itself is an issue – if power can only be held in order to give it away, to empower others – then the whole game changes.

Christendom is not on offer. The question for us now is in what ways we can live out our faith in the incarnation, in the eucharist, in the sacramental involvement of God in the whole world. What I'd like to go on to explore is what that might mean for Catholics in the Church in a postmodern society – when politics too has changed its meanings.

Postmodern politics

What does social action mean in a postmodern setting? It seems difficult enough to have any sense of what society is, let alone work out what might be done about it. Perhaps this is why the Catholic tradition seems to have splintered into so many diverse groupings: some maintain a traditional socialist view of what is to be done; but certainly in relation to active engagement they are a minority. Others look guiltily at those who seem so certain, without knowing how to resolve their own uncertainties.

'[T]he fundamental problem raised by processes of social change that are primarily external to the institutions and values of society . . . is that they may fragment rather than reconstitute society . . . Instead of social classes, we would witness the rise of tribes.'[18] Tribes are the curse of politics – I don't think it's too strong a statement. The essence of a tribe is of a mutual identification that overrides all other principles, in which the interest of the tribe is itself the greatest good. Of course, in postmodern times tribes are re-configured; they are not monolithic or static. People adopt tribes and leave them; they may even belong to different tribes in different aspects of their lives. But however fleeting they may be, the concept of identifying with a tribe undercuts the principle that is fundamental to a Catholic view of society, the principle enunciated in *Rerum novarum*, the Pope's 1891 encyclical which is viewed as the beginning of social teaching as a distinct aspect of Roman Catholicism – the principle that we are all one another's responsibility. 'Whatever you did to the least one of these, you did to me,' said Jesus.[19] Bishop Frank Weston said it in more flowery language: beyond any particular political programmes, it is of the essence of the Church's life that we are just as responsible for those unlike us, and those we don't like, as we are for those with whom we naturally gather.

The fragmentation into tribes is accompanied by another, even more quintessentially postmodern, disruption of society. Guy

Debord's *The Society of the Spectacle*[20] seems to express perfectly the distraction and apathy into which we have fallen; a channel-flicking mentality which is not prepared to make the act of commitment to anything that would result in any genuinely satisfying engagement, to change things within the individual or within the world. His first paragraph says enough: 'The whole life of those societies in which modern conditions of production prevail presents itself as an immense accumulation of *spectacles*. All that once was directly lived has become mere representation.'[21]

Any form of Christian community has to live differently from this. A community formed on a Catholic and incarnational vision cannot claim to retain either of those titles if it capitulates to individualist consumerism or tribalism. There's a danger here for any form of Christian community that depends on networking rather than geography as the basis of its congregation; I'll return at the end, though, to some ideas of what an authentically Christian 'tribe' might look like. But neither can we ignore those trends and tendencies, if we are to continue a real and constructive engagement with the wider world in the name of Christ.

As we have already observed, this modernist project of the balancing of rights and duties, of holding the tension of various needs and duties is no longer meaningful. People are beginning to think in a different language; no longer inclined to claim their rights from within the social framework, but regarding it as somehow outside themselves. Why not begin litigation against the negligent hospital, even if it means that the provision of health care in general is compromised for everyone, if you no longer feel connected to the needs of others?

Liberating theology[22]

The changes I have outlined have been reflected, sometimes unconsciously, in the 'theologies of liberation' that have grown up around the world. Liberation theologies developed in Latin America particularly, where the phrase comes from, as Christians – especially Roman Catholics who were members of poor and marginalized communities – began to explore the Bible for themselves, and found there a radically different gospel from the one they had heard in the Church's official teaching. The Jesus they met preached liberation, justice for the poor, and judgement on the rich. He told stories in ordinary language directed at poor peasants. He welcomed outsiders and criticized the religious establishment. People began to put all of this together with their own experience – and, most controversially in Latin American theology, with a Marxist critique of how their own societies worked – and started to challenge the quiet passivity with which they were officially encouraged to respond to injustice. In that context, 'liberation theology' had a clear meaning, referring to a tradition of dissident Roman Catholic theologians, who saw in the Marxist analysis of society – and the practice that followed, of seeking wholesale, even revolutionary, change – something which also expressed a Christian vision for the Kingdom of God. That form of liberation theology may not have much to do with the hierarchical and fundamentally conservative, reformist vision in traditional Catholic teaching, but it is a reaction against it within the same world, and sharing some of the same presuppositions. The problem is still conceived in terms of an assumed collectivity of people who seek justice as a whole. In postmodernism the danger is that tribes will seek victory, not justice – and that the self-centred individual will seek nothing more than entertainment.

Now there are multiple theologies of liberation, some growing out of the perceived continuing imperialistic tendencies of earlier forms. It's in that flowering of a variety of liberation theologies that I believe we can find a way into living the message of the gospel in postmodern society, but not on its terms.

Is theology in Britain the same as theology in South Africa? Can an interpretation of the Bible delivered in a Tudor church in Stoke Newington be expected to apply to a church in a shanty town on the edge of Manila? The assumption of the Church's theologians throughout most of church history has been that, however much they disagreed, their disagreements were about the same sort of thing, and that there was a right answer to be had. The truth was out there, and it was the theologian's task to mine it out, and then persuade everyone else that they'd got it right. Well, I was using the inclusive 'they' there, but actually it was almost always a 'he'. And almost always from the Western world, almost always from the educated classes, almost always white.

Liberation theologies challenge all of that, starting from the perspectives of Native American, black South African and Japanese Christians; growing from the experience of gay and lesbian people, or of Latin American women. But they have at least one common thread; theologies of liberation don't just try to replace other theologies – to push themselves to the top of the heap as the fashion of the moment, and then defend themselves against the next trend. That may be what happens, of course, but liberation theologians would argue that they are trying not to win the competition, but most importantly to change the rules of the game.

What happened first in Latin America (and has in many ways been effectively quashed by the consistent appointment of conservative bishops over many years) was also stirring in other parts of the world. The black spirituality of the USA began to mutate into a black theology which claimed that God was definitely committed to the struggle for liberation – that God was black, in the words of one famous writer.[23] In African and Asia, theologians began to critique the Western assumptions that had been imported along with Christianity into their cultures – and pointed out that Jesus was not after all a European. Feminist theologies articulated women's perspectives – and so it goes on.

These theological movements sprang from a common sense that God was on the side of those who were excluded, cut off from the mainstream, left out of the power mechanisms and the decision making. They were not, though, the same as each other – there is no such thing as 'liberation theology'; there are many diverse theologies of liberation.

So liberation theologies are contextual by nature – their method, content and structure emerge out of the situation in which they find themselves. Liberation theologians would argue that this is true of all theologies – including those that emerge from centres of power and privilege, and use their dominance to claim universal validity. So, while Latin American theologies of liberation have concentrated on re-interpreting human agency – the freedom of people within history to create their future – Native American theologians and feminists (from different starting points) have found it necessary to develop a new theology of nature and the world around us. Liberation theologies have also developed critiques of one another: thus, black women criticized male black theologians for ignoring the specifically sexist aspects of racist oppression. Lesbian and gay people criticized most of the existing forms of liberation theology as ignoring their situation.

But there is a real problem for those of us who regard ourselves as Catholic. If theology arises out of experience, is there any stopping point before we reach theologies that are constructed by each of us individually? If not, is there such a thing as the Church at all – what do we have in common? It's a possible extreme case of what Catholics have always accused Protestants of – allowing the theology of private opinion to take precedence over the Church's tradition.

Part of an answer to this criticism may rest in the concept of praxis: that one's social class or group's place within society is an essential component of theology. Liberation theologies therefore depend not on an individual experience but on that of a group, within the social and economic context in which it is placed. Theology happens, moreover, in the interaction of the community with its context: it's not something restricted to books and lecture theatres. So when a group of oppressed people concretely refuse to accept their oppression, theology is happening. For those people, new truths about God are being enunciated as much through their action as through their reflection. But still – are we condemned to theology as opposition? The people of Israel enacted a theology of praxis when they exterminated the people who were in the land before them, one might argue; how universal can a liberation theology be? Is it also good news for the oppressors?

Liberation theologies approach the past with suspicion. In order to construct a new just world, all that is old must pass muster – that is to say, the present experience of the community is the key tool for interpretation, and is dominant over all other sources of knowledge. Anglicans traditionally have acknowledged three sources of theological truth – the Christian Tradition, the Scriptures, and reason, which I would be happy to expand to include experience more widely. But there is I think a deliberate move in many liberation theologies to do away with this dialogue: Tradition and Scripture are useful only if they happen to be in agreement with experience.

Is theology always actually a reflection of our context? Of course, given where we've been already in this book, I would be inclined to answer 'yes'; there is nowhere we can stand outside our own concerns, background, prejudices and preferences. But it's not only that, and I think that's why Scripture and Tradition are non-negotiable. We need to have them interfering with our own perceptions in order to reflect more deeply on what it is that God is saying to us here and now. Paradoxically perhaps, it is only, I think, when we wrestle with those things that seem clearly wrong in the Scripture – like the violence of the Old Testament – that we are led beyond easy answers to our own problems.

Liberation theologies have grown up almost everywhere – except in the central places of power and influence in the world, which I suppose is understandable. I think that the impulse behind them, in their very multiplicity, is key for a new Catholic theology of social action. But we need to find a way of tying that up with an appreciation of Scripture and Tradition as more than resources to be drawn on when we agree with them – so that liberation theologies can fulfil their potential to bring to life our communities' understanding of themselves. The Church need not have the politicians' fear of remembering the past – or even of conceding that sometimes policy solutions can be found in revisiting the past rather than always needing to be seen as new.

Think Catholic, act local

In chapter 2 I talked about the incarnation as a language that went beyond power – God allowing Godself to be told in other people's words, in other people's stories. In chapter 3 I tried to spell it out a bit more, but mostly I was talking about power in the Church. Now we come up against what all of this new way of thinking means in the world at large. It's neither a capitulation to postmodern preferences, nor the adoption of one particular political method. What I'd like to suggest is not so much a political programme as a repertoire of actions – all based though on a clear and theological starting point. That starting point, as it has been for (particularly Anglican) Catholics for the last century, is the doctrine of the incarnation, but the incarnation as re-interpreted with this new language of power.

I'm not the first person to try this; I write in the shadow particularly of John Milbank (I may however be the first person to try it in ordinary English).[24] Milbank criticizes liberation theologies for being insufficiently theological – accepting a materialist critique of society as if it could be imported wholesale into theology. He also criticizes tendencies in Catholic social teaching that lead towards a right-wing, static and hierarchical view of society. He contrasts these with a perspective he calls 'gothic', which privileges those other places in society, between

the state and the individual, in which he argues human relations can flourish and justice can be founded.[25] Here he finds
a root for socialism which is more theological than that of the
liberation theologians, and a vision for the Church's teaching
which is more radical than the conservative tone of much
Catholic social thought (he is particularly anxious about the
pronouncements of the then Pope John Paul II).

> Multiple associations cease to 'mediate' between part and whole,
> but become themselves a new sort of context, a never 'completed'
> and complexly ramifying 'network', involving 'confused', over-
> lapping jurisdictions, which disperses and dissolves political
> sovereignty.[26]

I know I don't completely understand Milbank, and I'm pretty
sure I don't completely agree. But I love that sentence. I am sure
that we need what I understand by his description – networks
and groupings that do not seek to become logocentric centres
of power, but de-centre the existing power structures, unbal-
ance the forces of our age.

It is in the relationships of these groupings, and most
specifically when they recognize Christ in one another even
while disagreeing, that we see the incarnation worked out.
This directly contradicts the traditional understanding of the
Catholic vision, summed up in this quotation from Clement of
Alexandria: '[Jesus says:] Come unto me and gather together
as one well-ordered unity under the one God, and under the
one Logos of God.'[27] It's not the unity that's the problem, but
the assumption that unity means uniformity. If, as I'm suggesting, the Logos is not accessible to us as one definite whole, then
diversity is the only way in which it can be reflected (refracted)
in the world. We remain Catholic, because we have a vision that
encompasses the fact that God's work is wider and deeper
than our own vision of it. We also remain Catholic because we
are not committed only to the interests of our own selves, or
tribes, or even churches. The gospel is always for all people, and

especially those who are most rejected and written out of the story society likes to tell of itself.

I hadn't come across Trevor Huddleston's sermon when I first drafted the paragraphs above: now I feel both reassured, and slightly deflated, to realize I'm merely repeating what he had to say twenty-odd years ago. 'I would like to hope against hope that the Church of England might turn from its pre-occupation with its own structures, its own liturgical and doctrinal quarrels – even its own identity – and discover again a theology of Creation. That is the only challenge open to those who, today, would claim to be the heirs of the Oxford Movement: for it is a challenge to our Catholicism.'[28]

Huddleston urged an inclusive vision in which the Christian contribution is made alongside people of other faiths and none in working together for the good of the world. His perspective is I think more Catholic than those who argue that there must be a contrast between the different stories of human nature that different traditions tell.[29] The secular story doesn't necessarily undercut and contradict the Church's story. Nor does the Church have only one story to tell. There are many stories of Jesus, and the Church's job is to keep on telling them all.

The foundation of our story-telling should be that we walk in the footsteps of Jesus, who poured himself out for the world. That's one reason why Catholics do not need to have the same level of suspicion that most theologians of liberation do towards the Tradition and the Scripture. For all that they are influenced by human sinfulness in all its many manifestations, and have been used for all sorts of purposes, both Scripture and Tradition are also sacramental – they are means by which the Holy Spirit is present. Without being uncritical, we can still recognize that they call us to account as much as we them, and rather more.

Back in chapter 2, p. 28, I mentioned the idea of kenosis – emptying. Part of the quotation was this: 'Kenotic self-surrender is God's Trinitarian nature, and is therefore the mark of all his works "outwards" (the creation, reconciliation, and redemption of all beings).' I think it should mark us too – we should learn to live as 'kenotic communities'. That would then give us resources for engaging in action that a postmodern world could comprehend (even if it didn't like it).

It wouldn't be just changing the tactics while still having a fixed strategy – a hidden logocentrism. Nor would it be a sort of enthusiastic exodus from the present into an undefined promised land. Church communities, large and small, need to practise the undermining of the world's structures by living differently. It's not about our programmes, it's about our way of life.

A kenotically structured church community in this context knows that it is in Jesus, in his death and resurrection, that the hope of the Kingdom is realized. It also knows that it must live that message as Jesus did – by exposing itself in vulnerability to the world, by serving without expecting programmatic results, without a plan even for bringing in the Kingdom. That is in God's hands, not ours.

We can only do it – we can only keep on pouring love out, keep on being vulnerable – if we are also continually filled with the Spirit. There have been traditions in the Church before which have emphasized the Church's role in and for society, but which, without the same root in Tradition, have all too easily become somewhat spiritual caring agencies, not churches at all. The more we make our boundaries porous to the world, the more we must also return to the sacraments that make Christ present.

To think Catholic is to remain rooted in faith, in its unity in time and space, without (and this is where many would disagree) needing to require uniformity beyond the basics of the Catholic creeds. It is also to remain focused not on the Church (and we've been pretty bad at this) but on the world – the whole world – for which Christ died. That will require different responses at different levels – but the key word should be the local. What 'local' might signify, though, will vary widely. Just look at the way it's used in the Church: in Catholic thought the 'local' church is the diocese under its bishop. Only the most well-taught congregations will even consider that as a meaning of 'local'. But it is one of the most challenging and profound aspects of our faith that there is in the end no boundary to what is local, because we are called beyond the boundaries that people put up against each other. What is local for each community or person is the place in which they operate; a parish church must and should respond to the needs that come to it, first and foremost. But those needs are connected with everyone else's needs. As part of a diocese, each local community should be involved in the issues of its wider region. Skipping a few steps along the way, as part of the whole Church Catholic it should be considering the needs of the whole world.

Issues of industrial or agricultural change lead into issues of international trade; dealing with unwonted disasters leads to thinking about climate change. This is the meaning of one of the ugliest, but most useful, words I know, 'glocalization': local and global are part of the same thing. It makes some things much more difficult. The Church cannot just join in with a local protest that may be more reflective of local tribalism than genuine need. It's more dangerous; but, at a time when government initiatives seem to be incapable for all their good intentions of hitting the specificity of local issues, and are trapped in procedures and processes that stifle their life, the last thing the Church needs is programmes that model the same bureaucracy. The danger and risk of freedom is the key: the danger that people might get things badly wrong, the risk that it might not look good – that we might turn into another spectacle to titillate the public. But the way of safety is the way of death.

There's probably no way to avoid being a tribe of some sort, or at least being seen as one. But if the Church is to be a tribe, what sort of tribe would we be? What would a kenotic tribe look like? A tribe for other tribes? A contradiction in terms – exactly. The Church should be trying to turn inside out the individualism and tribalism that infect our political life, not by re-stating an authoritarian solution of right or left, but by living more deeply the life of its founder.

7

Lovable bodies

This chapter takes the form of a sort of case study. The issues of the ordination of women to the priesthood, and of human sexuality, have been so divisive that it has seemed impossible to avoid them. I've tried to think through what the principles I've been working on might mean for us as we face these issues that threaten to tear the Church apart.

This is the faith of the Church . . .

Before I was ordained, I had to go and see the Director of Ordinands, a priest whose responsibility it was to re-direct those who didn't really have a calling to ordination, and prepare the others for the selection process. I still remember something he said, which I didn't really understand at the time. Sometimes, he said, we say the Creed – and sometimes it says us. Well, he didn't put it quite like that, but what I got from him was a sense that faith didn't just depend on my own state at the time. Our own faith is our own, but it is also the Church's faith – which is more than just an accumulation of the individual commitment of all. The whole is much greater than the sum of its parts.

What that means for me is two things. First, on those days when faith is difficult and prayer seems meaningless, I can still say my prayers and the Creeds with a clear conscience, because I am not saying them merely as an individual, but as a member of the Church, and receiving the Church's faith when my own is lacking. But, second, it also means that the Church as a whole takes responsibility for things – and has the competence to do so. It's more than a democracy (though hopefully not too much less), because the Church is called as a body to discern the movement of the Holy Spirit.

This claim is made most forcefully of course by Roman Catholics for the teaching authority of the Pope, as Peter's successor the divinely inspired interpreter of the faith. I do not think that being an Anglican Catholic means I have to accept the Roman Catholic view of the Church's authority, because then I can accord none to my own. But nor does it mean the Church is purely a human institution. So – and this really isn't very postmodern – by signing up to be a member of the Church, I am also signing up to recognize that, in all its imperfection, the Church is nevertheless one of the ways in which God is at work in the world. A brief glimpse at church history, and all the things people have tried to use the Church for, convinces me all the more that God must have been at work, otherwise the whole thing would have collapsed centuries ago.

But here we come back to perhaps the deepest ambiguity at the heart of the Anglo-Catholic tradition. Anglican Catholics have been very keen on obedience to the Church in general terms, but rather less keen on the specific act of obeying. The Papalist position – that the Church of England was an accidentally detached part of the Church of Rome – was a great resource in this. If an Anglican bishop forbade something, appeal could be made to the fact that the Roman Church allowed – or even commanded – it. This appeal had the convenient aspect that since the Roman Catholic Church did not regard Anglican priests as genuinely ordained, there was no chance of real obedience being demanded from the people to whom it was supposedly owed.[1] This ambiguity was convenient for Anglo-Catholics for a long time, but it has come back to bite us with the controversies particularly over the ordination of women to the priesthood. For myself, the idea that the common mind of the body of believers as a whole (even when expressed in the Church of England's General Synod) is also part of the work of the Holy

Spirit has become a powerful resource in thinking about what it means to live a Christian life.

When it comes to ethical issues, issues that affect our own lives, the individualism of postmodernity comes through most strongly. It's really hard work even to think that the Church might have anything to say about personal morality – whether that's ethical consumption, justice in the workplace or, most of all, sexual behaviour. But it's this interplay between the individual conscience and the collective that can jolt us out of our own prejudices into something deeper. The big difference in a postmodern context comes from the very different attitude I've been suggesting towards power. The Church should not claim the power it has in fact never had, to coerce individual's souls. But that doesn't mean that all the power gets handed to each individual. When it comes to living together in one body, one Church, we have to find ways of making decisions. We'll probably never be very good at discerning the movement of the Holy Spirit, especially when the Spirit disagrees with us, but we have to try. And part of that is accepting that decisions with which we disagree have nevertheless some call on our loyalty as members of the body. We aren't called to abandon our own disagreement, but neither may we enthrone it as absolute – unless we disagree so radically that we can no longer, in conscience, remain within the same Church.

I don't want to go on about the ordination of women to the priesthood in the Church of England, though it's now a critical issue again as the Church creeps up very slowly on the possibility of ordaining women as bishops. There are many who regard themselves as Catholics in the Church on either side of that division – and one of the most tragic ways in which the division has poisoned the Church is that on each side there are those who are prepared to write off those on the other side as not really Catholic. I'm afraid it seems quite clear to me. On the one hand, all of us who are Anglican Catholics have to confront our ambiguity towards our own Church, and decide whether we really believe it is a true branch of the Catholic Church. If it is, it can decide whom it will ordain. If it isn't, in my view it has no authority to ordain anyone, male or female, or therefore to claim to be a place in which the sacraments are duly administered. But – and this is important – within that acceptance of the Church's decision the Church's response must then be to make as much space as possible for those who disagree. What we need is a dynamic of mutual care, not a competition for victory over one another. So, just as those in favour of women's ordination (mostly) refrained from breaking the rules before the decision was made, without changing their minds, so those who are opposed should not be expected to change their minds, nor to deny the reality of the change that has been made. And those of us who rejoice in the ordained ministry of women should express our love for those who disagree by refraining from making their lives more difficult, and by working together for the gospel which runs a lot deeper than these differences. But it is difficult to work together in a Church when some within it do not really accept it as fully a Church. Vatican II spoke of other bodies as 'ecclesial communities', not feeling able to confer on them the title of 'Church' because they did not share in the fullness of the Church's life. That's fine from a Roman Catholic perspective, but to believe it of one's own 'ecclesial community' is not in the end a tenable position. The constant flow of Anglo-Catholics into the Roman Catholic Church, from Newman onwards, has shown that amply enough. Even those who remain do so in an increasingly uneasy and unstable place.

The place of straight men in the Church

Now we come to the really thorny bit – the stuff that's tearing the Anglican Communion pretty much straight down the middle at the moment. It's about the minority who forget they are: the minority of straight men who have been used to running the show for so long that it's been taken as natural – so natural that lots of women and gay men have accepted it too. OK, so that's one starting point, which will annoy those who take their patterns of church organization from the New Testament (though I would deny such a thing is possible). And it opens up some of the divisions we're working with, and how deep they go. Where are our sources of truth? Some within the Anglican Communion want to relegate Tradition and reason/ experience to an invisible role. I'd argue that in doing so they tend to empower them more, as unacknowledged arbiters of 'what the Bible means'. But that's the way these arguments go – as often as not, around in circles of competing starting points.

Of course, I've got no problem in admitting that my perspective is partial, that I am influenced by many different factors, some of which I'm not aware of, that I can't claim to have the whole truth at my fingertips. The difficulty is that some seem to have no such difficulty in relation to their own positions of faith: rejecting the whole postmodern premise, they are sure that they have absolute foundations of truth that are not open to question. But we've been living with that tension for a long time. Conservatives have been accusing people like me of not really believing in anything, and my sort have accused the other lot of being blinkered fundamentalists. Neither true, but a lot easier than conducting a seminar on epistemology.[2]

What seems to have happened now is that this deeper division on how we know what's true has been put together with concern about the liberalization of Western society (i.e., one of the manifestations of postmodernity), and the specific issue of how the Church responds to homosexual people who believe that they can live out their sexuality as faithful Christians. We live in a society that is becoming steadily less obsessive about sexual behaviour. This is a matter of extreme concern to many in the Church, who find it a clear sign of moral decline, and respond by reinforcing the importance of right opinions about sexual behaviour and orientation. Just as I didn't get into the specific issues of women's ordination, nor am I going to rehearse any of the specific debates about homosexual practice. Partly this is a deliberate ploy in order to disappoint those readers who have turned straight to this chapter in order to find out how unsound I am, but mostly it's because I think the most important thing about these issues of sexuality, in a postmodern Church, is not so much the moral perspectives adopted as the way in which sexuality has become a shibboleth.

Sexuality is bound up with the question of the body, the physicality of ourselves. Western culture has been characterized as deeply ambivalent about, if not hostile to, the body, and much of that heritage has remained within the Church as it has been abandoned in society at large. It has been an unquestioned fact of religious discourse that bodies are less than spirits, that it is the spirit which is released from the body at death, that the earthly side of ourselves is the repository of all that is sinful and keeps us from God. Some of the seeds of this may lie in the New Testament, though it is not necessary to read Paul's interpretation of 'the flesh' in that way,[3] but it's not exactly unusual, except in postmodern Western society. So just as society at large is beginning, with some difficulty and prudery, to move away from fear of the physical into a wider understanding of what it means for human beings to be bodily, embodied, inseparable from the physicality of existence, the issue has become a fixation among the churches, leaving many in our wider society more and more convinced that the Church is composed of people living on some strange and unpleasant planet.

Just in order to make the point that this isn't only about homosexual behaviour, it is equally inexplicable to many Roman Catholics not only that gender can continue to be a bar to priesthood, but also that celibacy can be required of the clergy. It seems to me as an outsider to be a genuine question as to whether the Roman Catholic Church will choose the death of its priesthood, at least in the developed world, before it can bring itself to look again at these issues: and when the choice is put as starkly as that, it seems extraordinary that discussion of the issue is not even allowed.

An obsession with the sexuality of worshipping bodies, and the things they are or are not allowed to do, not only cuts the Church off more and more radically from the society it seeks to serve, it also cuts off one of the avenues in which the Church, and particularly its more Catholic traditions, has something to offer that could help to weave community and solidarity. As I have experienced it, Catholic worship is worship with the body: genuflections, crossings, standing, sitting, kneeling at various points, processions, and then the intimately physical actions such as kissing the cross at the Good Friday liturgy, or the washing of feet on Maundy Thursday. To be sprinkled with water as a reminder of one's own baptism, and continual need of renewed forgiveness, is for me far more powerful than reciting the Ten Commandments any number of times. But bodies are profane, unclean, unsafe; they do not do what they're told, they don't think the right thoughts, they are diffuse, confused, fallible. Bodies are postmodern things; modernism famously was more attracted to machines.

So the Church has problems at three levels. First, the problem some have with postmodernity as such, which is especially symbolized by issues of control, and bodily control in particular – and is also bound up in the question of truth: how certain can we be? Second, there's the problem of how people now think about the Church, the problem of authority: how much are we willing to accept any constraint on our own personal beliefs? Third and last, there's the issue this is supposed to be all about: what sort of sexual relationships are OK for Christians? It's no wonder then that a quite disproportionate level of significance has been given to the third question, because it's standing in for numbers one and two as well. It was interestingly illustrated in a letter sent recently by members of the Church of England's General Synod in support of a bishop who wants to remove his diocese from the Episcopal Church in the

USA, which denounced the whole Episcopal Church as being in the thrall of 'universalism and unitarianism'.[4] An interesting couple of accusations. To describe 'universalism' (the belief that all people will be saved – that hell is empty) as a heresy is a powerful move. The Church has contained many universalists for many years, but it has been seen as a cause of disagreement, not division. Now we seem to be moving into a period when any non-trivial theological disagreement is enough to justify splitting off from one another. The other accusation, 'unitarianism', states that the Episcopal Church no longer believes in the Trinity – at the least. Unitarians began as believers in God, who did not believe that Jesus was divine or that the Holy Spirit was a separate person in the Godhead. Many now don't believe in God at all. I'm not aware of this being the position of the Episcopal Church, but it does wonderfully demonstrate how attitudes towards certain issues, especially ones on sexuality, are being taken as markers of a much broader disagreement, one in which those on the other side are no longer regarded as Christians at all.

I think the conservatives are right that the issues at stake are deeper than mere ones of sexual conduct. I think they're wrong in assuming that those with whom they disagree are generally happy to throw out any bits of Scripture or Tradition they don't fancy that day. (Some may be, but not enough to make it a justifiable accusation.) What we're struggling over is what it means to live in postmodern times – whether we like them or not; what it means to be one Church together; and what we really believe about the created order: is it good or not, is it primarily fallen or primarily blessed? No wonder we're in trouble. And people who are both Christian and attracted to others of the same gender as themselves, are bearing the brunt of it all. That's definitely unfair. Catholics are most conflicted of all. It isn't exactly a secret that a good number of the Anglo-Catholic clergy are gay. All those who don't feel called to celibacy of course struggle with how they can reconcile their own sense of what is right and good with the Church's present position, which is that those who are ordained should have sexual relationships only within heterosexual marriage. Some struggle again with reconciling their own desires – and sometimes practice – with a theological agenda that is anti-modernist and very clearly sets out that all homosexual activity is sinful.

The positions are so entrenched that no-one can even claim to stand in a neutral place – if they do, there'll be thousands of people looking for evidence that in fact they lean one way or the other. Many of those involved in the debate wouldn't accept the starting points of this book – that is, they would disagree about what theological knowledge we have, and how we get it – and the disagreements would go on from there. But I hope at the least that I can repeat the steps that have been important in getting me to the place I'm now at.

The first ones are about bodies: are they basically good or bad? Is our first instinct to discipline or to celebrate? I think what I've said already leads to two conclusions. The first is that the incarnation is a sign of God's blessing of all that God has made, a commitment to the created order that does not deny its fallenness but does deny that sin can set the agenda. Bodies, and what they are created for, are part of God's plan, even the passionate messy bits. The second is that the Church is not called to try (even if it could) to exercise a coercive authority over its members. We are called into a relationship of radical equality, in which the relation of the whole to the part is continually in negotiation. The Church's sense of being guided as a body should, in a perfect world, cohere exactly with the individual discernment of all the members of the body. If that happened, we'd be in heaven already. In the meantime, the dynamic of using power for one another rather than over against each other suggests that the only real form of discipline is self-discipline: externally imposed punishment is never to be sought or chosen. I admit that it might be inescapable – but only when the integrity of the body as a whole is threatened.

That's all the more true because of the next step: what does it mean for us to live in unity? The Church's unity is important in itself, not merely as a by-product of being in agreement. It is part of our calling to be one, but – and it is a big but – that oneness is only really Christ-like when it is the unity of those who disagree. I think that's what it means for the Church to be diverse – a whole paradigm shift from the language of diversity as used in secular culture. In our society as a whole, 'diversity' signifies the obligation to recognize the sameness that underlies all differences of gender, ethnicity, sexuality, (dis)ability and so on. Very good. But in the Church, our diversity should I think be shown in the love we continue to feel for those with whom we disagree radically about what is most precious to us, the gospel of Jesus. Yes, of course there are boundaries – and I would suggest that the Apostles' and Nicene Creeds might serve us quite well.[5] They set out a framework of faith capacious enough to include a huge variety of practice and belief. When we try to set our boundaries more narrowly than that, I believe we are not purifying but mutilating the Church of Christ. 'Disagreement without division' is another way for me of describing the first traditional 'mark' of the Church, its unity. So we cannot ever seek division as a way out of our differences; it can only be forced on us when we are no longer able to say the Creeds together.

From all that I've said, it follows of course that no one person or group is in a position easily to say when someone else no longer 'really means it' when saying the Creeds. If my fellow Christian claims to believe, the first, second and third response must be to believe that person and remain in fellowship. When might I agree that individuals or groups have to be excluded, despite their own protestations, and even when they don't explicitly deny the Creeds? I suppose when an aspect of their belief or behaviour is so much out of sync with the Creeds that the claim just isn't plausible any more. That's where we run up against the buffers: I would point towards the behaviour of Christians who supported the Nazis, or apartheid, but not those who are lesbian or gay. It just doesn't strike me as a first-order issue, one over which we should break communion with one another.

Perhaps – just perhaps – if the issue of sexuality was disentangled from the other things of which it is part, the question of how we respond to postmodernity, and how we think about the Church, the questions of truth and authority I've been struggling with all through this book, we might just get somewhere. But now I'm going to go on to annoy almost everyone with some thoughts on how we might do it.

Paul's theological method in the modern world

As one of those who believe that there's nothing wrong with homosexual people expressing their love for each other in a sexual way, you might not think I'd be too keen on St Paul. After all, his denunciations of homosexual behaviour in his letter to the Romans are the most unequivocal and difficult to avoid of the rather small number of references in the Bible. But this issue isn't about counting verses. If it was, the re-marriage of divorcees (which Jesus describes as adultery[6]) would be far more of a dividing line between Christians. As it is, we seem to stay together across that issue without even thinking about it. What I'm interested in is theological method.

Paul felt called to take the good news of Jesus Christ to the Gentile world – an urban-based, Greek-speaking culture, whose religion consisted of the observance of the old Greek and Roman gods (Zeus and his family), with a good dose of emperor worship, which was developing at this time as the Roman emperors began to get increasingly elevated views of themselves. It couldn't be more different from the rural, Jewish, monotheist environment in which Jesus had preached and worked wonders.

The biggest problem was the Jewish Law. The Law set out what it meant to be Jewish: in order to convert to Judaism, observance of the Law was the way. Since this involved circumcision as a starter for male converts, it wasn't an easy road. Jesus had clearly obeyed the Law himself, and certainly many early followers of his never even thought that there was any other alternative. Matthew's Gospel, which, so far as any of the Gospels does, reflects the viewpoint of Jewish believers, has Jesus saying 'not one stroke of the pen . . .'.[7] Paul took all of this and turned it inside out. He didn't deny that the Law was God-given, but he reflected deeply on the most startling and challenging aspect of Jesus' teaching – also set out particularly strongly in the Sermon on the Mount – which intensifies the demands of the Law beyond anything that can be legislated, into the depths of the human heart. If even feeling angry is the same as committing murder, what help for any of us? So Paul develops his theology of the Law as a vehicle for revealing to us our sinfulness, the tutor that brings us to the place we need to be, admitting that we need a new life in Christ.

So suddenly the gospel becomes something that still challenges the Gentile people of the Eastern Mediterranean, just as much as it did Jesus' original hearers – but no more. They are called to repent, to accept the new life of Christ, to give up their worship of the old gods and – dangerously – of the emperor. But they don't have to become Jews. Paul's brilliant theological transmutation of the gospel retained the heart of its demand, but equally brilliantly extricated the gospel from the danger of its identification with one particular faith and social setting. The Holy Spirit was most definitely at work.

We would probably all agree on that, but not so much on the next suggestion I want to make. For me, the Holy Spirit was at work more in the theological method than in the specific content of Paul's theology. I talked earlier about the way in which the presence of God is given over into the world of our interpretations, about the humility of God allowing us to be at work in such an active way in constructing faith. What we see happening in the New Testament is the first stage of that process, one that we are invited to join in. Paul's theological synthesis is the first word, not the last – we should be doing what he also did.

So when we come into the era of postmodernity (leaping 20 centuries forward), we aren't called just to repeat Paul's prescriptions, standing firmly against postmodernity as the Church did against modernity until it was almost finished. We're invited by the Holy Spirit to find the resources in Jesus' gospel that will enable us to make the same challenge to transformation now that he did in first-century Judea.

If that's how we relate to postmodernity, the denunciation of 'liberalism' is attacking the wrong thing. It may well be that parts of the Church are going too easy on contemporary culture, just as others may be too negative. But denouncing each other is not the response: we need to listen to one another's perspectives and compare them back against the gospel – against the Scripture and the Tradition. We may keep on disagreeing, but if we all agree that we are trying to do the same sort of thing – trying to let the gospel speak in our contemporary situation – then there's an underlying unity which can hold us together. So (perhaps) those of us who are 'liberal' (oh, how I hate that label) could accept that those who are 'conservative' are attempting to bring the gospel to bear on contemporary culture – and, maybe with more difficulty, the reverse could apply as well.

If that were combined with a basically positive attitude towards bodiliness, and a real commitment to the sort of diversity I talked about before, and a rejection of attempts to coerce one another – well, flying pigs would be sighted all across the Anglican Communion. Peace might also break out. But in order to remain in peace, we need to think a bit more about the practicalities of unity in real diversity, and this is where I'll annoy a few more people.

How to walk as a group

A group naturally goes at the speed of the slowest member of the group, divided by the number of people in the group. There are many million Anglicans, and a significant number of them don't want to move at all. Not a pleasant prospect for those of us who love racing ahead.

The danger with a scenario like this is that it is always the innovators who are open to the accusation that they are abandoning the faith for new-fangled doctrines. Paul faced that problem too. The difficulty is that, though it might be true, it also undoubtedly true that those who continue merely to repeat last year's (or last century's) solutions are also abandoning the faith. They are not handing on the faith, they are denying the creative work of the Holy Spirit by claiming that everything is set in stone – a stone that is normally suspiciously like the radical innovations of one or two generations ago.

In order to walk together, those naturally at each end of the group – the front and the back – need to swallow their impatience or their suspicion, so that each can remain in touch with the other. Not that everyone needs to move at the same pace, but there needs to be a connection linking the whole pilgrimage together – a connection primarily of trust that we are all heading in the same direction, but almost as importantly of information, so that those at each end really know what the concerns are of those at the other.

This is of course all about method – it applies just as much to other areas of the Church's life as to issues of sexuality. Those who are experimenting with new ways of doing liturgy, those who are planting new churches in unusual places, are all at different leading edges – and might well number themselves among the conservatives in other respects. There is no monolithic vanguard, nor rearguard. There is one body (still, at the moment). We continue to need each other – and particularly those we feel least desire to be with – if we are to witness to the unity that Christ brings across all possible boundaries.

8

Living the life you love

On enjoying being human

The Church is far better at feeling anxiety and fear in the face of human existence – and especially the messy bits to do with gender and sexuality – than it is at celebrating its essential goodness. But that's where you have to start, in an incarnationally centred theology. In Jesus Christ a human body is glorified to the heart of God: as St Athanasius said, following other early church teachers: 'God became human so that we might become God.'[1] It's that close a relationship we're invited into. It is that celebratory starting point which is at the heart of a renewed Catholicism. The earthly has been raised to the heavens, so the things of this earth are just as much God's care and delight as the 'spiritual' things that are often dissociated from them. It goes for politics and church life, as we discovered in the last chapter – and it goes just as much for the personal lives of women and men. As you know, part of my own spiritual pilgrimage has been a movement from the evangelical to the Catholic wings of the Church of England. I was brought up in a conservative evangelicalism in which (it seemed to me) faith was primarily an intellectual exercise, of being convinced of the truth through persuasive argument, and making a decision for faith primarily through conviction at that level. Bodies were a bit of an embarrassment, continually needing to be controlled so that they didn't interfere with the really important business of the spiritual life. I hasten to add that this is how it affected me, which may not be at all what it was or is like for those still within that part of the Church.

I then moved through a charismatic phase, in which rationality definitely took a back seat, and it was the inner experience of the Spirit that was most important. This is much more than merely emotion, and there are aspects of it that are still part of my own spiritual life, but it was a way of worship that seemed to induce a high degree of stress among those who weren't sure they were getting it right. For some, charismatic worship is a release into enjoyment of the body in a way they had felt was previously impossible in worship. Certainly there was lots more movement, but for me it connected more with anxiety than freedom. If you sat still, it was a sign that you were afraid of what the Spirit might be doing: raising hands and all the rest became a sort of liturgical norm, a demonstration of conformity more than inspiration. For me, it was difficult to maintain real engagement with the experience of the community unless there was some intensity of feeling, of being moved; laughing or weeping were OK, but being bored was not. When the emotion ran out, did that mean the Spirit had departed? Had I been an anxious sort of person, that might have been a hard time, but as you know I tend rather towards the self-assured, so I packed my bags and left, returning to the less pressured environment of the Church of England.

So when I eventually found it, the Catholic tradition came as a great relief, because for me it meant a freedom from the impossibilities of always thinking or feeling the right things. I knew I never had, and I rather suspected a lot of other people didn't either, but it would be taboo to start a conversation about it. Finally I found myself somewhere in which faith was more a question of what one did: the body disciplined the unruly emotions and reason by inculcating the habits of holiness. And, moreover, there was a theology that backed up this valuation of the bodily, which regarded the church's worship and the life of the

Christian in the world as equally joined up in a celebration of the sacramental action of God in the material world.

But – as well as getting into the Catholic tradition, I was being much affected by writers like Derrida (yes, him again). That also had a profound effect on my spirituality, because it wasn't just an intellectual pursuit but one that affected the whole of me. I'm not the only one: quite a few people have written about the connection between Derrida's writings and religion, not least Derrida himself in his later years.

When Derrida himself came to the subject, he quite clearly dissociated himself from the theological tradition that seemed to many people to connect up quite obviously with his work. The apophatic tradition is the current in Christian spirituality that can never rest content with anything that is being said of God, being acutely aware that God lies beyond all definitions, words or pictures that we might use. Derrida's continual questioning of any certainty that we might claim in making statements about God seems to be just like this: but he pointed out that the apophatic tradition still moved towards, in Graham Ward's words, 'a grand unveiling of a single, generative principle'.[2] That is exactly what Derrida's work ceaselessly undercuts: the attempt to communicate the essentially incommunicable, that which goes beyond what can be put into words. Apophatic spirituality *is* continually saying 'no' to whatever words are used to describe God, but it does so precisely because stripping away all of that makes the unclouded vision of God possible. For Derrida 'there is no place from which to observe "the nakedness of God" '.[3]

Derrida places a warning in the path of any theology that pretends to describe God in a direct way. But his work does not thereby *become* a theology of its own. Nor is it an atheist manifesto. In my own spirituality, the writings of people like Jacques Derrida have enabled me to be comfortable with a spirituality based not on knowledge – nor on the lack of knowledge – but on relationship. But, as you will understand, it is difficult to describe without trying again to do the impossible, to place God within a human framework.

Nevertheless, I began this book by writing quite a lot about myself, and I'd like to end by trying to link that story with the whole pattern I've been trying to weave in this book. I'd like to talk about why it is that the Catholic tradition really works for me – about spirituality, prayer, and the sense of what it means to (try to) live a whole life. It may not be the very heart of my spirituality, which I wouldn't know how to tell you about, but it provides a way in, a path that leads in the direction of God, at least as I have met God.

Telling the story of yourself

I talked earlier about recovering the concept of the Church as a body in thinking about how to be neither a 'solid' nor a 'liquid' sort of institution. A body is organically inter-connected; each part responds to the needs of any other. It is the complete naturalness of the life of a body that is our aim, though we know we will not attain it until the Kingdom comes.

But most of us know we won't attain it till then in our own bodies either. We are a mess of conflicting emotions, desires and needs, and it's a life's work to create a self that is a cause more for rejoicing than shame. It has been my experience of the Catholic tradition that it has given me the shape for living in a way that leads to joy. For me, the Catholic tradition has provided a way of integrating aspects of my faith that were previously slightly disconnected from what I felt was most truly 'me'. As you'll have gathered by now, I haven't given up on an intellectual approach to faith, and neither have I switched off my emotions, having passed through my conservative evangelical and charismatic experiences. But I now experience them as a part of my faith which is also part of the whole of me.

In approaching this chapter, I have been enormously helped by reading Charles Taylor's magisterial book *Sources of the Self*.[4] If Derrida is the bouncer on the door of the nightclub of the Spirit, I've found in Taylor a skilled bartender, providing just the right stimulant to make the experience take off. I've taken from him a way of understanding how my own spiritual experience, my sense of obligation to others, and my sense of what makes life worthwhile, all interlock through the matrix of a Catholic engagement with faith. Taylor's book is subtitled *The making of the modern identity*; it's a book of philosophy and history, not theology. But his vision of what it means to have a properly rounded sense of self resonates deeply with a Christian view of human beings.[5] The reason I find him so congenial, I think, is that he links up the aspects of being human that I found in Catholicism, though I hadn't been able to articulate them until I read Taylor: '. . . one might try to single out three axes of what can be called, in the most general sense, moral thinking. As well as . . . our sense of respect for and obligation to others, and our understandings of what makes a full life there is also the range of notions concerned with dignity.'[6]

The way in which he links one's own personal sense of worth, one's way of living in society, and one's sense of 'the good' (of God), showing that they are necessarily inter-related, speaks to my understanding of the communal, political, consensual nature of the Church as I have been explaining it – and to my place as an individual within it. My own story, like everyone else's, can only feel as if it's heading in a coherent and fulfilling direction if it's also at the same time part of a story that goes wider and deeper, but without obliterating or denying my own individuality. Or as Taylor puts it: 'I have been arguing that in order to make minimal sense of our lives, in order to have an identity, we need an orientation to the good . . . Now we see that the sense of the good has to be woven into my understanding of my life as an unfolding story.'[7] The narrative of my own life, it turns out, isn't just a useful narrative device for getting a book going, or even a gesture of honesty – it's an essential part of any story I want to tell about the things that really matter more widely, about how we live together in society or in the Church. If my own story isn't also part of that wider story, the result will be internal discord and inauthenticity in my public life. Our understandings of what is 'the good', our understandings of ourselves, the stories we tell of our lives and our vision of human society all evolve together, and (ideally) strengthen one another.[8]

But does Taylor's approach not also contradict everything I've argued up to now about postmodernity? I think not (obviously) – and this is why. I've argued all along that the 'deep postmodernity' of Derrida, far from leading to the nihilistic consumerism that is often called postmodernity, actually provides the Church with resources to engage with it and live an alternative. That's why it has been so important for me to stand out against the individualism of postmodernity, even while wanting to embrace much else within it. That illusory freedom prevents us from finding true human flourishing, because it detaches us from everything we need in order to grow. We need to be planted somewhere; we can't continually uproot ourselves to see if another flower bed has a better view, and still expect to thrive. But, unless the Church accepts the challenge of postmodernity, unless we learn the humility of knowing we can't describe or control God, unless we learn to use power for each other rather than against each other, we will never become a place in which people can thrive in all the diversity God wishes.

Taylor's concept of the 'orientation to the good' resonates for me with what I experience as the mystery of faith, that we are called beyond anything we can demonstrate or prove. In that experience, I find myself (at least in my own view) somewhere on the same ballpark as Anthony Thiselton, the evangelical theologian and most definitely not a fan of postmodern thought. He suggests that 'acting in the present on the basis of that which is yet to be proven or "seen" constitutes a faith that has world-transforming and self-transforming effects. It transforms the self because, like the experience of resurrection, it *reconstitutes self-identity* . . . The self perceives its call and its value as one-who-is-loved within the larger narrative plot of God's loving purposes for the world, for society, and for the self."[9]

I expect Professor Thiselton and I might have some disagreements about how certainly we can know God's narrative – and also about what some of it might say. But for me, that second point is not a problem; it illustrates the undesirability of trying to tie down the gospel. Once I was able to embrace my own radical inability to know God, I was able to enjoy having a relationship with God, through the 'narrative' of the Catholic tradition. To return to Taylor:

> A vision of the good becomes available for the people of a given culture through being given expression in some manner. The God of Abraham exists for us (that is, belief in him is a possibility) because he has been talked about, primarily in the narrative of the Bible but also in countless other ways from theology to devotional literature. And also because he has been talked *to* in all the different manners of liturgy and prayer . . .
>
> A sense of the good finds expression not only in linguistic descriptions but also in other speech acts – as with the example above of prayer. And if we follow this example further, into liturgy, we see that expression goes beyond the bounds of language as normally and narrowly conceived. The gesture of ritual, its music, its display of visual symbols, all enact in their own fashion our relation to God.[10]

Taylor is giving an example in order to explain his general argument, but it felt to me reading the passage above that he was also telling my own story. If the story I've been telling is to make sense for you (if you want it to become part of your story), then you'll need too to find connections between your own individual, interior life and the story of the Church.

Trying to live it

I've quoted already a couple of times Michael Ramsey's statement that 'Individualism has no place in Christianity, and Christianity, verily, means its extinction,'[11] and it's to that that I would like to return in this chapter, focusing as it does on the individual – on me, to start with, but hopefully also on you.

To be anti-individualist is to be as counter-cultural as one can be. You will have realized by now that I don't think my sources among the postmodern thinkers necessarily promote individualism – for all that they are clearly opposed to the traditional ways in which power has been exercised in society, at every level. But there is still a real question, which I have touched on in thinking about how the Church works, about how authentic human living happens in postmodern times in a way that is neither individualistic nor authoritarian.

Authenticity – there's that word again. I bet some of you are wondering how I can possibly use it as if I agreed with it. After all, authenticity as presently used is completely tied up with the individualistic and narcissistic culture of self-fulfilment. But here Charles Taylor comes to the rescue again: in *The Ethics of Authenticity* he points out that this is not a necessary connection. There is a way of thinking about authentic individual living that is not integrally related to the relativism promoted in postmodern culture.[12]

Taylor points out that the notion of authenticity develops as the locus of connection with 'the good' – for us, God – moves away from an external authority source, and becomes internalized. This is the very opposite of the internalization that Foucault describes, in which it is exactly that external authority which is internalized (though were he alive he would probably disagree). This vision of personal authenticity is not a mere internalization of external authority, but a discovery that it is through our deepest inner selves that we encounter the source of our selves.

The important part of Taylor's argument for me is that this turn inwards does not necessarily imply that it is illegitimate for anyone else to have any influence over my actions. An authenticity that has its roots in my own connectedness with myself and with God does not necessarily mean that freedom has to be completely self-determined too.

Taylor then points out a fact also made in a completely different way by Derrida: that we are not in fact on our own, even in our innermost thoughts. We are always using language, even when we are not speaking, because we think using language. Or, as Taylor says, 'it would take a great deal of effort . . . to *prevent* our identity being formed by the people we love'.[13]

If we are to have meaningful lives at all, we cannot construct them without being in relationship. We cannot make meaningful choices unless we have some sense of how and why some choices are better than others – and that sense of worth cannot be generated out of the individual alone. 'I can define my identity only against the background of things that matter. But to bracket out history, nature, society, the demands of solidarity, everything but what I find in myself, would be to eliminate all candidates for what matters.'[14] For Taylor, Derrida and Foucault 'cannot but exalt and entrench anthropocentrism'[15] – that is to say, their philosophy inevitably sets up the philosopher as the arbiter of meaning, while disqualifying anyone else's attempts to speak meaningfully. But that only applies if there is a self who is the undeconstructed deconstructor: if the philosopher (or anyone else) can inflict deconstruction on the world, without being subject to it him- or herself. On the other hand, if we are all involved, it is individualism that becomes meaningless, whether from Derrida's perspective or Taylor's.

So if we are to be authentically individual, we must also be connected to that which makes our lives meaningful. And that connection cannot be in the mode of a hierarchical authority, which would deny our own freedom. In fact it has already been expressed in another of the ancient Christian paradoxes: 'it is no longer I who live, but Christ who lives in me. And the life I live now in the flesh I live by faith in the Son of God, who loved me and gave himself for me'.[16] So in order to tell most meaningfully the story of myself, I find myself telling the story of Jesus. And in doing that, I cannot avoid telling the story of Jesus' body, which is the Church. And so, if I am to be myself, I cannot avoid the challenge of living alongside my brothers and sisters in Christ, and paying attention not just to my own wishes but to theirs as well. And not being in a position definitively to say that I know the truth – as no-one can – it is those with whom I disagree to whom I need to pay particular attention, in case they are revealing a truth I am trying to avoid. It's hard – and I certainly don't feel qualified to judge others – but our personal spirituality has to be in some sort of creative relationship with the way in which we worship and seek to serve society.

Letting God be

My own spirituality, then, is only my own when it is shared; it becomes deeper as I become more deeply involved in the life of God, which is also through the Holy Spirit the life of the Church. But that doesn't answer the question of what it means for each of us in our own lives to live that celebratory incarnational faith I was describing at the beginning of the chapter. Maybe we know now that the key note of a Catholic spirituality should be joy – joy in the love of God shown in the incarnation of Christ, joy in the goodness of the creation of which we're part, joy in the sacramental life of the Church, joy in our own hearts. But that doesn't make it happen. What I'd like to do now is to look at some of the routes of joy that have worked for me, in addition to the liturgical life of the Church at worship. I'm sure it'll be something else that works for you, but maybe this will help you to work out what that might be.

But having started with joy, I do have to face up to the fact that Catholic spirituality has a reputation for being extremely good at inducing guilt. Large parts of it have been built on a hatred of the body, with flagellations, hair shirts and other forms of self-inflicted pain seen as signs of holiness. There were lists of sins to consider before attending confession, and of course the penances to undergo afterwards. The problem I think is not with the recognition of our sinfulness, but with the way in which sin was so often identified with the body, and particularly with sex – and the impression that life was just a continual battle against sin, not a gift to be enjoyed.

John O'Donohue spoke of the 'sin of the unlived life'[17] – a deeper level of sin than the 'sins' that can be placed on lists, condemned, confessed, healed. It is that inner disturbance which causes outer disturbance; sinfulness has its root in the ways in which we are prevented, or prevent ourselves, from living the lives that we could. The spiritual life is not (should not be) a place of condemnation or of conformity, but of exploration and adventure. O'Donohue spoke of the need to focus 'not on the will of God but the imagination of God'. Spirituality focused on God's will, he said, all too easily becomes a spirituality of denial, of attempting to re-create oneself in conformity to certain rules. Spirituality focused on God's imagination, God's creativity, is something else again. It's an invitation to find ourselves as God's beloved and to start to live that life.

Letting God be in us is an invitation to freedom and creativity. Personally, I'm not one for painting, and still less for doing stuff with clay. When I see anything advertised as 'spirituality through creativity', I run. But creativity is at the heart of my spirituality, though it doesn't involve getting the playdough out. For me, the creativity that connects me with the creativity of God goes through words and silence, not making or doing. For others it comes through physical work, or through contemplation of nature, or through activity. Creativity is something that happens within ourselves, not the name for a certain set of activities.

God's creativity and ours

Taylor points out that the notion of authenticity can be traced back to St Augustine, 'who saw the road to God as passing through our own reflexive awareness of ourselves'.[18] The truest form of authenticity, then, is to live perfectly in the love of God. Which leads me straight back to St Augustine again, and one of his famous sayings (with a little more context than usual):

> A father beats a boy, and a boy-stealer caresses. If you name the two things, blows and caresses, who would not choose the caresses, and decline the blows? If you mark the persons, it is charity that beats, iniquity that caresses. See what we are insisting upon; that the deeds of men are only discerned by the root of charity. For many things may be done that have a good appearance, and yet proceed not from the root of charity. For thorns also have flowers: some actions truly seem rough, seem savage; howbeit they are done for discipline at the bidding of charity. Once for all, then, a short precept is given you: Love, and do what you will: whether you hold your peace, through love hold your peace; whether you cry out, through love cry out; whether you correct, through love correct; whether you spare, through love do you spare: let the root of love be within, of this root can nothing spring but what is good.[19]

I thought it was worth including the longer quotation to make the point that Augustine is not talking about niceness when he talks about love. He writes in the context of illustrating that the truly loving act may not be apparently the most pleasant. I suspect most of you reading this will agree with me that beating children is a bad thing, but the point remains valid. The love that Augustine is advocating is the love of the Son who sacrificed himself for the salvation of the world. It is love lived out in this spirit – and only through the Holy Spirit – which is free from all other rules.

Here is the freedom of real creativity; the more we live immersed in the love of God, the freer we are to follow our instincts, which God is making holy. Anyone can see of course how dangerous that can be, what a justification for all sorts of dreadful behaviour – unless we are constrained by the love of the Christian community around us, pointing us away from our own self-deceit and in the direction of love. It's not easy to live that way – in fact it's nearly impossible. It needs the support of the Church's sacraments and prayer. It certainly can't be done without time and space given to refreshing ourselves, and returning to the centre of the Holy Spirit's life within us. So it's to those resources for the individual spiritual life that I want to turn now.

Round and round and round we go

It is not knowledge that is at the heart of prayer, but a relationship without words which cannot be expressed in words. Not being able to know sets me free to love.

Let me point to what I mean through just one example of something that's been important in my own spirituality: walking the labyrinth. It's a form of spirituality that is obviously bodily – it's about movement, walking. But before I go any further, a few words about labyrinths. They are not mazes; you can't get lost. A labyrinth in the sense I'm using has only one path, leading to the centre, but it goes in all sorts of directions before it gets there.[20] I first encountered a labyrinth in San Francisco, where there is one laid out on the terrace outside Grace Cathedral (there's now one inside too). Grace Cathedral is nearly at the top of the hill – and San Francisco's hills are *steep*, so there's a great sense of the air around you as well as the city below. Walking the labyrinth (I discovered afterwards) is supposed to comprise three stages. As you walk in you let go of those things that hinder your own wholeness and your relationship with God. After experiencing the peace and prayerfulness of the centre, the journey back out, retracing your steps, is a time to re-connect with yourself, with your neighbours, with the world. Well, sort of; I didn't really do anything like that at a conscious level, but I think that does reflect quite a lot of what was going on for me. The labyrinth made a space within which I could be free, in the very act of freely submitting to its way of being. There was nothing to prevent me striding straight to the middle, no hedges or 'labyrinth guardians' waiting to tell me off. It was in accepting the walk around and around, taking some long while to get somewhere I could walk to in five seconds – and, with slightly more difficulty, accepting the long walk out again as well – that I also opened a door in myself to the presence of God. It was literally a useless activity: it had no use that could be measured; it was unprofitable. It was in ceasing to have to be useful or profitable that I was able to be free to God.

I have come across other labyrinths since, and they've had the same effect. There was a very wet one, cut into the grass in the garden of Burford Priory in Oxfordshire, when I was on retreat there. There was one in a space normally used as a bar, at Greenbelt in 2006. It's not the surroundings or the environment, though, but the action which is the important thing. The 'labyrinth offers us the possibility of being real creatures in symbolic space'.[21] That is, it's a space in which the boundaries can become blurred between this world and the Kingdom of God.

Living the life you love

Van Morrison famously sang, that if the life you're living is one that you love, you will receive blessing from above. I've been trying to show why the Catholic tradition, as I have understood it, is for me a way of finding out what the life I love is like, and then having the resources to live it. My hope is that it might be that for you as well. And that's it. Nothing more to say right now, except to leave you with a favourite quotation of mine, which was also a favourite of that great Anglo-Catholic and saint, Archbishop Michael Ramsey, from Irenaeus of Lyons in the second century: 'the glory of God is a human being fully alive'.[22] And, finally of all, a quotation from the present Archbishop, Rowan Williams, who in meditating on that phrase expresses the hope on which this book is founded:

> The point of the Church, if you like, is that glory may dwell in our land . . . the glory of God in transfigured human faces, and we are there to hold that space and that hope, that place for the imagination to go.[23]

Notes

1 It's my story

1 G. K. Chesterton, *The Everlasting Man* (London: Hodder & Stoughton, 1925), 288.

2 Harry Williams, in *Poverty, Chastity & Obedience* (London: Mitchell Beazley, 1975), 13, quotes (with no reference) John Oman: 'Strictly speaking, no book was ever written except in the first person, and it is not modesty to say, "This is merely my opinion on my limited experience", for no human verdict on anything was ever more.'

3 'Mornington Crescent' is a spoof game played on the BBC Radio 4 show *I'm Sorry, I Haven't a Clue*: for the purposes of this illustration I am following the common assumption that there are no rules at all, but the contestants suggest different London place names, pretending all the while that this is a game with the strategic sophistication of chess. (Exhaustive research indicates that places other than London Underground stations are acceptable.) The 'winner' is the one who reaches Mornington Crescent.

4 Geoffrey Rowell, *The Vision Glorious: Themes and Personalities of the Catholic Revival in Anglicanism* (Oxford: Oxford University Press, 1983).

5 Someone pointed out that I should introduce Kenneth Leech, rather than assuming everyone knows who he is. Ken is an Anglo-Catholic Anglican priest and Christian socialist. He founded Centrepoint, which became the United Kingdom's leading national charity tackling youth homelessness. He's a prolific author, and he co-founded the Jubilee Group, for 30 years the standard-bearer of Anglo-Catholic Socialism.

6 Kenneth Leech, 'The Renewal of Social Vision: A Dissident Anglo-Catholic Perspective', in *The Anglo-Catholic Social Conscience: Two Critical Essays* (London: Jubilee Group, 1991), 1–11, 2.

7 K. E. Kirk, 'Truth', in *Report of the Oxford Movement Centenary Congress, July, 1933* (London: Catholic Literature Association, 1933), 28–36.

8 Kirk, 'Truth', 29.

9 Kirk, 'Truth', 30, 31.

10 Michael Ramsey, *The Gospel and the Catholic Church* (London, Longmans, 2nd edn, 1956), 38.

11 Leech, 'Renewal of Social Vision', 4. He quotes the late Valerie Pitt's article 'The Oxford Movement: A Case of Cultural Distortion?' in Kenneth Leech and Rowan Williams, eds, *Essays Catholic and Radical* (London: Bowerdean, 1983), 205–23, quotation at 223.

12 O. Chadwick, *The Victorian Church Part 1* (London: SCM Press, 1987; 1st edn, 1966), 196.

13 A process begun by the Sexual Offences Act 1967; full equality was granted only through the 2003 Act of the same name.

14 Donald Gray, *Earth and Altar* (Norwich: Canterbury Press for the Alcuin Club, 1986), *passim*.

15 Kenneth Leech and Rowan Williams, Editors' Introduction to *Essays Catholic and Radical*, 7–10, 7.

16 Frank Weston, *Our Present Duty*, concluding address to the 1923 Anglo-Catholic Congress (London: Society of SS Peter & Paul, 1925), 11, 12.

17 George Carey, 'Revitalizing the Catholic Tradition', in Jeffrey John, ed., *Living Tradition* (London: Darton, Longman & Todd, 1992), 17–28, 18.

18 Rowell, *The Vision Glorious*, 247.

19 Kirk, 'Truth', 34.

20 There's a good run-down of the various incarnations in Michael Johnston's article 'Where Two or Three Are Gathered', at <www.anglocatholicsocialism.org/familytree.html>, accessed 13 Jan. 06.

21 Richard Holloway, 'Behold, I Make All Things New', in Jeffrey John, ed., *Living Tradition*, 115–30, 128–9.

2 My other story: Postmodern *and* Catholic

1 H. H. Kelly SSM, *Catholicity* (London: Student Christian Movement, 1932), 32–3.

2 Greenbelt is a Christian-based arts and music festival which has now been running in Britain since 1974; it's also a sort of annual meeting place for many of the alternative worship groups. See <www.greenbelt.org.uk> – and if you haven't been, go!

3 Cathy Kirkpatrick, Mark Pierson and Mike Riddell, *The Prodigal Project: Journey into the Emerging Church* (London: SPCK, 2000), 61–2.

4 Jean François Lyotard, *The Postmodern Condition: A Report on Knowledge* (Minneapolis: University of Minnesota Press, 1984), xxiv.

5 Charles Gore (1853–1932) was successively Bishop of Worcester, Bishop of Birmingham and Bishop of Oxford, and a leading figure in the Christian Social Union: a cautious socialist, but an inspirer of more radical figures.

6 Charles Gore, *The Anglo-Catholic Movement Today* (London: Mowbray, 1925), 7.

7 We'll come back to this in the next chapter, when I talk a bit about Zygmunt Bauman's book *Liquid Modernity* (Cambridge: Polity Press, 2000).

8 Gore, *Anglo-Catholic Movement*, 7.

9 Gore, *Anglo-Catholic Movement*, 7.

10 There are many books by and about Jacques Derrida, and many of them are nearly impossible to read. If you want to take the next step into the labyrinth, may I suggest Graham Ward's essay 'Deconstructive Theology', in Kevin J. Vanhoozer, ed., *The Cambridge Companion to Postmodern Theology* (Cambridge: Cambridge University Press, 2003).

11 Jürgen Moltmann, 'God's Kenosis in the Creation and Consummation of the World', in J. Polkinghorne, ed., *The Work of Love* (London: SPCK, 2001), 137–51, 140–1.

12 John Habgood, *Catholicity: The Michael Ramsey Memorial Lecture* (Durham: St Mary's College, University of Durham, 1990), 1–2.

13 John Habgood, *Confessions of a Conservative Liberal* (London: SPCK, 1988), 90–1.

3 Power and how to lose it

1 Umberto Eco, *The Name of the Rose* (London: Secker & Warburg, 1983).

2 Trevor Huddleston CR, 'On National Apostasy', *The Times*, 15 July 1983.

3 Matthew 7.29.

4 I wish I could find this story again, so I could give the author's details. If there's ever a second edition, maybe someone will be able to let us know so we can get it right.

5 George Orwell, *1984* (London: Everyman, 1992; 1st edn 1949), 311.

6 Manuel Castells, *End of Millennium* (Oxford: Blackwell, 1998), 378.

7 A note from Wikipedia for those who haven't come across Castells: 'Manuel Castells is a sociologist, particularly associated with research into the information society and communications. According to the Social Sciences Citation Index's survey of research in 2000–06, Castells was ranked as the fourth most cited social sciences scholar and the foremost cited communications scholar in the world.' <http://en.wikipedia.org/wiki/Manuel_Castells>, accessed 29 Jan. 08.

8 Michel Foucault, *Discipline and Punish* (New York: Penguin, 1979; original French edn 1975), 3–6.

9 Zygmunt Bauman, *Liquid Modernity* (Cambridge: Polity Press, 2000), 126.

10 Bauman, *Liquid Modernity*, 76.

11 Jorge Luis Borges, 'The Lottery in Babylon', in *Collected Fictions* (New York: Penguin, 1998), 101–6.

12 Bauman, *Liquid Modernity*, 135.

13 Found at <www.haloscan.com/comments/dstpfw/117132761675830099/>, accessed 5 Jan. 08.

14 Stephen Moore, *God's Gym: Divine Male Bodies of the Bible* (London: Routledge, 1996).

15 Moore, *God's Gym*, 123, quoting *New Webster's Dictionary*.

16 K. E. Kirk, 'Truth', in *Report of the Oxford Movement Centenary Congress, July, 1933* (London: Catholic Literature Association, 1933), 328–36, 34.

4 Churches and their priests

1 N. Boyle, *Sacred and Secular Scriptures: A Catholic Approach to Literature* London: Darton, Longman & Todd, 2004), quoted in Timothy Radcliffe, 'The World Shall Come to Walsingham', in Philip North and John North, eds, *Sacred Space* (London: Continuum, 2007), 65–79, 77, no original page no. quoted.

2 E. Mascall, *Christ, the Christian and the Church* (London: Longmans, 1946), 121.

3 Michael Ramsey, *The Christian Priest Today* (London: SPCK, 2nd edn, 1985), 109, 111.

4 Tradition with a capital 'T'! Here's the definition from the *Catechism of the Catholic Church*: 'Sacred Tradition and Sacred Scripture, then, are bound closely together, and communicate one with the other. For both of them, flowing out from the same divine well-spring, come together in some fashion to form one thing, and move towards the same goal. Each of them makes present and fruitful in the Church the mystery of Christ, who promised to remain with his own "always, to the close of the age"'. Where I would not agree with Roman Catholic teaching is in the idea that the Tradition can only be authentically interpreted by the Magisterium: the Pope and bishops in communion with him.

5 Pete Ward, *Liquid Church* (Carlisle: Paternoster, 2002).

6 John Maynard Keynes, *The General Theory* (New York: Harcourt Brace & World, 1964), 383.

7 Terry Pratchett, *Making Money* (New York: Doubleday, 2007), 226.

8 Dietrich Bonhoeffer, *Letters and Papers from Prison* (Eng. enlarged edn, London: SCM Press, 1971), 360.

9 Michael Ramsey, *The Gospel and the Catholic Church* (London: Longmans, 2nd edn, 1956), 38.

10 K. E. Kirk, 'Truth', in *Report of the Oxford Movement Centenary Congress, July, 1933* (London: Catholic Literature Association, 1933), 28–36, 34.

11 <www.quaker.org.uk/Templates/Internal.asp?NodeID=93328 &int1stParentNodeID=93929&int2ndParentNodeID=89813&int3rd ParentNodeID=89813&strAreaColor=orange>, accessed 5 Jan. 08.

12 Zygmunt Bauman, *Liquid Modernity* (Cambridge: Polity Press, 2000), 172.

13 Ward, *Liquid Church*, 91.

14 Bauman, *Liquid Modernity*, 156–7.

15 Though this isn't an area I know very much about, it may be that new ways of being church have much to offer priests serving multi-parish rural benefices, in which the traditional style is still expected at one level, but is also experienced as deeply unsatisfying, both for congregations and priests.

16 Bauman, *Liquid Modernity*, 155.

17 See L. William Countryman, *Living on the Border of the Holy* (Harrisburg, Penn.: Morehouse, 1999).

18 *The Methodist Worship Book* (Peterborough: Methodist Publishing House, 1999), 288–9.

19 T. S. Eliot, 'East Coker', in *Collected Poems 1909–1962* (London: Faber & Faber, 1974), 201.

20 Zygmunt Bauman, *Intimations of Postmodernity* (London: Routledge, 1992), xxii.

21 Romans 12:6.

22 Margaret Wheatley, *Leadership and the New Science* (San Francisco, Calif.: Berrett-Koehler, 1999), 89.

23 Wheatley, *Leadership*, 39.

5 God's joyful work: Worship

1 *Vatican Council II: The Conciliar and Post Conciliar Documents* (Leominster: Fowler Wright, 1975), 9.

2 'Tridentine' refers to the Council of Trent, at which the Roman Catholic Church restated its doctrine and reformed its liturgy in response to the Protestant Reformation. It took place between 1545 and 1564 (with a few breaks); the liturgy remained substantially the same until the Second Vatican Council in the 1960s. Some development was perhaps overdue.

3 A. G. Hebert, ed., *The Parish Communion* (London: SPCK, 1961; first edn 1937).

4 Hebert, 'The Parish Communion in Its Spiritual Aspect', in *The Parish Communion*, 3–29, 3.

5 Brother Edward, ed., *Sunday Morning, the New Way* (London: SPCK, 1938); J. M. Nicholson, *The Family Service (About the Parish Communion, no. 1)* (London: SPCK, no date).

6 'Christian liturgy is primarily a celebration of God's action and, only secondarily, a response of the church, an action of the people of God.' Kenan Osborne OFM, *Christian Sacraments in a Postmodern World* (Mahwah, NJ: Paulist Press, 1999), 161.

7 Alexander Schmemann, *For the Life of the World* (Crestwood, NY: St Vladimir's Seminary Press, rev. edn, 1973; 1st edn 1963), 139–40.

8 Gregory Dix, *The Shape of the Liturgy* (London: Dacre Press, 2nd edn, 1945), 744.

9 See chapter 2, page 28.

10 As summarized in Osborne, *Christian Sacraments*, 169–77.
11 Justin Martyr, *First Apology*, 67.1, in R. C. D. Jasper and G. Cuming, eds, *Prayers of the Eucharist: Early and Reformed* (New York: Pueblo, 1987), 30.
12 *Patterns for Worship* (GS888) (London: Church House Publishing, 1989), 18–20.
13 *Liturgiam Authenticam: On the Use of Vernacular Languages in the Publication of the Books of the Roman Liturgy* (London: Catholic Truth Society, 2001).
14 Jonny Baker and Doug Gay, *Alternative Worship* (London: SPCK, 2003), 33–4.
15 There's a great summary of his thought and writings at <www. infed.org/thinkers/ et-schon.htm>, accessed 5 Nov. 07.
16 Donald Schon, *The Reflective Practitioner* (New York: Basic Books, 1983), 68.
17 Schon, *Reflective Practitioner*, 138.
18 Why not have a look at <www.alternative.worship.org> if you're not sure where to start.
19 Pete Ward, *Liquid Church* (Carlisle: Paternoster, 2002), 113.
20 Matthew 13.52.

6 Left a bit, left a bit: The Church political

1 From Percy Dearmer, *Socialism and Christianity* (London: Fabian Society, 1907). Found at <www.anglocatholicsocialism.org/ dearmer.html>, accessed 16 Feb. 08.
2 Kenneth Leech and Rowan Williams, Editors' Introduction to *Essays Catholic and Radical* (London: Bowerdean, 1983), 7–10, 9–10, quoting Maurice Reckitt in 1933, no reference given.
3 Geoffrey Rowell, ed., *Tradition Renewed: The Oxford Movement Conference Papers* (London: Darton, Longman & Todd, 1986).
4 Trevor Huddleston CR, 'On National Apostasy', *The Times*, 15 July 1983.
5 Emmett Jarrett, ' "Behold I am doing a new thing": mysticism and politics in contemporary Christianity', in Leech and Williams, eds, *Essays Catholic and Radical*, 81–94.
6 Leech and Williams, Editors' Introduction to *Essays Catholic and Radical*, 9.

Notes to pages 96–108

7 Frank Weston, *Our Present Duty*, concluding address to the 1923 Anglo-Catholic Congress (London: Society of SS Peter & Paul, 1925), 11, 12.

8 K. E. Kirk, 'Truth', in *Report of the Oxford Movement Centenary Congress, July, 1933*, (London: Catholic Literature Association, 1933), 30.

9 Kenneth Leech, 'The Renewal of Social Vision: A Dissident Anglo-Catholic Perspective', in *The Anglo-Catholic Social Conscience: Two Critical Essays* (London: Jubilee Group, 1991), 4.

10 Donald Gray, *Earth and Altar* (Norwich: Canterbury Press for the Alcuin Club, 1986), 93, quoting the Revd Lewis Donaldson, a leading Christian Socialist at the turn of the twentieth century.

11 John Orens, 'Priesthood and Prophecy: The Development of Anglo-Catholic Socialism', in Leech and Williams, eds, *Essays Catholic and Radical*, 158–80, 166.

12 Orens, 'Priesthood and Prophecy', 166.

13 Orens, 'Priesthood and Prophecy', 168.

14 C. Marson, 'The Social Teaching of the Early Fathers', in A. Reid, ed., *Vox Clamantium: The Gospel of the People* (London: A. D. Innes & Co., 1894), 198–224, 201.

15 *The Return of Christendom. By a Group of Churchmen* (London: G. Allen & Unwin, 1922).

16 Gray, *Earth and Altar*, 227.

17 <http://sacramentalsocialists.wordpress.com/>, accessed 8 July 08.

18 Manuel Castells, *End of Millennium* (Oxford: Blackwell, 1998), 383.

19 Matthew 25:40.

20 Guy Debord, *The Society of the Spectacle* (New York: Zone Books, 1995; original French edn 1967).

21 Debord, *Society of the Spectacle*, 12.

22 In what follows I have especially used Susan B. Thistlethwaite and Mary P. Engle, eds, *Lift Every Voice: Constructing Christian Theologies from the Underside* (Harper & Row, 1990).

23 James Cone, most famously in *A Black Theology of Liberation* (New York and Philadelphia, Penn.: Lippincott, 1970).

24 Milbank is at the time of writing Professor of Religion, Politics and Ethics at the University of Nottingham, and a formidable thinker and writer.

25 John Milbank, *The Word Made Strange* (Oxford: Blackwell, 1997), 275.
26 Milbank, *Word Made Strange*, 276.
27 Quoted in William T. Cavanaugh, 'The City: Beyond Secular Parodies', in John Milbank, Catherine Pickstock and Graham Ward, eds, *Radical Orthodoxy* (London: Routledge, 1999), 182–200, 183.
28 Trevor Huddleston CR, 'On National Apostasy', *The Times*, 15 July 1983.
29 As Cavanaugh does for instance in the article cited in note 26.

7 Lovable bodies

1 In 1896, Pope Leo XIII issued *Apostolicae Curae*, an examination of Anglican ordination rites which led to the famous conclusion that 'The ordinations carried out according to the Anglican rite have been, and are, absolutely null and utterly void' (sec. 36).
2 Epistemology is the philosophy of knowledge: e.g., how do we know what's true or false?
3 I'm not exactly up to date with this reference, but it's the one that first made me think of this: John Ziesler, *Pauline Christianity* (Oxford: Oxford University Press, rev. edn, 1990), esp. 77–9.
4 Letter to the Church of England Newspaper, 7 November 2007, accessed at <http://www.anglican-mainstream.net/category/common-cause/page2/> 10 July 08.
5 In the Church of England, at any rate, the Apostles' Creed is generally said at Morning and Evening Prayer on Sundays and at baptism services, and the Nicene Creed at the Eucharist.
6 Matthew 5.32.
7 Matthew 5.18.

8 Living the life you love

1 Athanasius (ed. and trans. A Religious of CSMV), *On the Incarnation (De Incarnatione Verbi Dei)* (London and Oxford: Mowbray, 2nd edn, 1953), 93.
2 Graham Ward, *Barth, Derrida and the Language of Theology* (Cambridge: Cambridge University Press, 1995), 53.
3 Ward, *Barth, Derrida*, 254.

4 Charles Taylor, *Sources of the Self* (Cambridge: Cambridge University Press, 1989).
5 Which isn't all that surprising, of course, since he is a Roman Catholic.
6 Taylor, *Sources*, 15.
7 Taylor, *Sources*, 47.
8 Taylor, *Sources*, 105.
9 Anthony Thiselton, *Interpreting God and the Postmodern Self* (Edinburgh: T. & T. Clark, 1995), 160.
10 Taylor, *Sources*, 91–2.
11 Michael Ramsey, *The Gospel and the Catholic Church* (London: Longmans, 2nd edn, 1956), 38.
12 Charles Taylor, *The Ethics of Authenticity* (Cambridge, Mass.: Harvard University Press, 1991), *passim*, but see esp. 25–6.
13 Taylor, *Ethics*, 34.
14 Taylor, *Ethics*, 40.
15 Taylor, *Ethics*, 61.
16 Galatians 2.20.
17 John O'Donohue, 'Imagination as the Path to the Spirit', CD GB07.050, Greenbelt Festivals 2007.
18 Taylor, *Ethics*, 27.
19 Augustine, Homily 7 on the First Epistle of John, sec. 8, accessed at <www.newadvent.org/fathers/170207.htm>, 11 Jan. 08.
20 There's loads more about labyrinths at <www.labyrinth.org.uk/>, accessed 11 Jan. 08.
21 Rebecca Solnit, *Wanderlust: A History of Walking* (London: Viking, 2000), 70.
22 Irenaeus of Lyons, Adv. Haer. IV.
23 <www.archbishopofcanterbury.org/sermons_speeches/060504%20Chelmsford%20clergy%20address.htm>, accessed 11 Jan. 08.